INTERRACIAL RELATIONSHIPS BETWEEN

BLACK WOMEN *and* WHITE MEN

CHERYL Y. JUDICE

Printed in the United States by Bookbaby

7905 North Crescent Blvd.

Pennsauken, NJ 08110

info@bookbaby.com

Cover design by: Rocio Martin Osuna, Graphic Designer

Madrid, Spain

rociomartinosuna@gmail.com

Special thanks to Janelle Joseph for her editing assistance

Most names and identifying details have been changed to protect the privacy of individuals

Print ISBN: 978-1-54393-416-8

eBook ISBN: 978-1-54393-417-5

To my husband, Hecky Powell, whose love and unstinting support made my research and this book possible; and,

To the black women and white men who crossed the racial divide to pursue loving relationships

TABLE OF CONTENTS

PREFACE

Have you ever wondered what it is like for an African American woman or a white man to date or marry interracially today?

If so, this book will provide some insights.

Black women are the one group of women least likely to marry, or to marry outside of their race. There are many reasons for this, some explored within this book; nonetheless, romantic relationships between black women and white men are becoming more commonplace.

This book contains vignettes on the lives of black women who are dating, married to, or divorced from white men. Black women and white men in interracial relationships were interviewed between 2014 and 2017 to learn how they met and how their relationships progressed. These forty interviews offer thought-provoking insights on the lives of those willing to cross the racial divide in pursuit of personal happiness.

This book does not include the experiences of black men who are married to white women. There are several resources on this topic, including my 2008 academic text, *Interracial Marriages Between Black Women and White Men,* published by Cambria Press and available online or in libraries.

INTRODUCTION

Black women are the only group of women in America who cannot take for granted that if they seek marriage to a black man that there will be an ample supply of available men from which to choose. This is not a new problem; indeed, it goes back several decades, but there hasn't been much public discussion about how to resolve this issue. It is almost as if the plight of black women looking for eligible partners is the elephant in the room. Unlike issues related to skin color, hair texture, and low self-esteem, it is more difficult for black women to talk about it publicly to draw attention to the problem. I am tired of meeting so many women who have suffered in silence and simply given up on having someone love them for who they are. I am writing this book because I have seen firsthand the sadness confronting many black women who have never experienced a fulfilling romantic relationship. To be sure, many of these women lead productive and fulfilling lives without ever marrying. Some even decide to have children without husbands, but a common theme I have observed among many is a wistfulness for a part of life which has been denied them...a part of life other groups of women take for granted.

I have set out in this book to explore the lives of black women who have chosen to cross the racial divide in their quest for personal happiness.

Most young girls grow up fantasizing about dating and marrying someone within their own racial/ethnic group, and indeed, approximately 87% of marriages in the U.S. are between people of the same racial/ethnic backgrounds. Black girls growing up today face a very different reality, as illustrated by a few daunting statistics. First, black females begin to outnumber black males by age 16; for whites, this does not happen until approximately age 32 (1). Second, black men are more than twice as likely as black women to marry outside of their race (2), black women are the least likely group of women to marry outside of their race (3). Third, for every 100 college-educated black females, there are approximately thirty-five to forty comparably educated black males (4). These statistics underscore a sobering reality that sets the parameters for this book.

I became interested in the dating and marriage prospects of young black women thirty years ago. Living in Evanston, Illinois, I met numerous middle to upper middle class black families residing in several North Shore communities. These couples supplied their children with the privileges that their social and economic status afforded while living in predominantly white suburban areas. Recognizing that their children might feel somewhat isolated growing up in majority white suburbs, many of these families joined black social groups or black churches to expose their children to a broader African American culture. What happened to many of these children as they entered their teen and early adulthood years differed based on gender. Young black males who might be considered physically attractive enjoyed a broad range of friends across race/ethnicity and gender and had active social lives. On the other hand, young black females, while they may have had strong friendships with white females, were not as likely to have equal numbers of white male friendships. Moreover, for some black females, as the dating years began, former friendships with white females began to fade. In sum, the social experiences of this group of black males and females took dramatically different routes as the teen years ended.

Fast forward to the late 20s and early 30s for this group of young African Americans, and the following had occurred: Most of them had completed college; many were enrolled in or had completed professional, graduate, or trade school, and/or were beginning their careers. Some in this group were involved in romantic relationships, but it was only the black males who were engaged or had married. Their black female counterparts were single, an often-voiced concern and the subject of conversation, particularly among their mothers. Many of these black mothers expressed their frustration about the dating and marriage prospects of their daughters, while the black mothers with sons noted that the males were pursued by women from various racial/ethnic groups. Now in their late 40s, it is not surprising that many of the black males eventually married outside of their race or were involved in long-term relationships and had children, while the black females either remained single or married much later in life (late 30s to early 40s). Moreover, some of the black women who eventually married were the second wives of their black husbands, often becoming stepmothers and/or married to men who were not from the middle to upper middle class in which they had grown up. Only one of the black males who married outside of his race was married to a woman who came from a lower socioeconomic background and none married women who had children from previous relationships.

My anecdotal observations of the dating and marriage patterns of middle class black children who grew up in Chicago's predominantly white North Shore suburbs thirty years ago are not unique. Numerous conversations with middle class black families living in similar circumstances around the country confirmed my observations, although in more recent times, some of the distinctions in dating and marriage patterns that I initially observed have begun to diminish. Succinctly, middle class African Americans often experience different dating and marriage patterns, leaving black females with fewer dating and marriage options if they only seek partners within their racial/ethnic group.

The primary purpose of this book is to tell the stories of black women who are dating, married to, or divorced from white males. Recognizing that the marriage pattern of black women married to white men represents the smallest number of interracially married couples, and the most extreme end of the marriage spectrum, it is my hope that presenting their stories will cause more black women to intentionally seek to broaden their idea of suitable dating and marriage partners. This book is not intended to diminish black males, only to present another dating and marriage option for black women who wish to get married and who recognize that the continuing numerical imbalance between black men and black women in this country reduces the likelihood of marrying within their racial/ethnic group.

Second, this book gives voice to white men who are dating, married to, or divorced from black women. Their stories and perspectives provide balance to those of the women.

Finally, the narratives in this book are limited to the dating and marriage lives of heterosexual middle class African American women and white men who crossed the racial divide in their quest to achieve personal happiness. Additionally, I interviewed ten black women who are divorced from their white husbands. Sixty personal interviews were conducted for this book. The majority of interviews were with black women currently married to white men, half of whom were interviewed with their husbands. Eleven interviews were with black women who were dating white males or who had been in relationships with white men, and five were with white males exclusively without their black girlfriends or wives. The majority of participants were between the ages of 21 and 55 and were interviewed from 2014 through 2017. It is my hope that the stories found within these pages will be thought-provoking and provide insight on what it means to interracially date or marry.

CHAPTER 1

BLACK WOMEN AND DATING CHALLENGES

For most young people, the college years represent the last time in their lives they will be in an environment comprised primarily of their peers. Attending college is viewed as a part of the American dream for many young people, the first chapter in their lives as independent adults and the last educational milestone to be achieved. For students living away from home, college life provides them with the freedom to date and form relationships, and to explore their sexuality without necessarily being constrained by parental boundaries. Most U.S. colleges and universities strive to achieve diverse student populations, which exposes some students for the first time to living or working in close proximity to people from various racial/ethnic groups and sexual orientations. Indeed, one of the primary goals of attending college is to explore and expand one's interests and to participate in new experiences.

For young African American women, attending college may mark the first time they realize that there are far fewer black males enrolled in school than black females. This numerical disparity impacts the social lives of both sexes, often resulting in tension between and within the two groups. Earlier generations of young women often chose to attend college for an additional reason—the possibility of finding one's future husband. College campuses have long operated as social meeting grounds, and many young women enrolled at certain schools based on the type of young men who also attended. In the past, there was little shame in working on one's 'Mrs.' while completing one's bachelor degree. Feminists of the late 20th century ridiculed the notion that young women would attend college to find prospective spouses, but the idea was resurrected in 2013 when a 1977 Princeton alumna, who had met her husband while a student there, wrote a letter to the *Daily Princetonian* exhorting the women students to look around campus for a future husband before graduating. Ms. Patton wrote, "Here's what nobody is telling you: Find a husband on campus before you graduate." Ms. Patton went on to say that her letter "was just intended to suggest to these women who are on campus today, again, keep an open mind. Look around you. These are the best guys…If the women's movement has done what it was supposed to do, it should enable all women to make whatever choices are appropriate for them, even if their choices are seemingly retrogressive." (5) While her letter was met with mixed reactions, Ms. Patton does make an important point—college campuses provide the last concentrated arena for young adults to meet each other.

I suspect many black female co-eds wish that they could follow Ms. Patton's advice while in college. Across the nation, more women are enrolling in college than men, and when you factor in race/ethnicity, black women are at a sharp numerical disadvantage if they only seek black males to date. The following example illustrates the devastating social consequences of the numerical sexual imbalance.

A few years ago, I was invited to speak on a panel at a university seminar on dating and marriage with two other sociologists who study race, class and gender issues and one licensed marriage counselor. The large audience was comprised primarily of African American graduate and undergraduate students. Most of the questions were fairly easy for the panelists to respond to, until one young black woman stood up and, in an emotionally anguished voice, began to speak. She stated that she was a junior in college, and in the three years she had been in school she had never been asked out on a date, and she had other girl friends in the same circumstances, and that she never thought when she went to college she would not have much of a social life, and that no one would want to date her. She was worried this same pattern was going to continue once she finished college, and wanted some advice on how she could change this situation.

The room became uncomfortably quiet and the panelists were struck by the young woman's pain. Once she sat down, the other panelists began to suggest ways in which she could meet new people and perhaps through them find other people to socialize with, eventually meeting prospective dating partners. Time ran out before I could ask the young woman who she considered as potential dates, but it was clear from her responses to the other panelists' suggestions that she was focused on finding a suitable black man. The seminar ended and I didn't have the opportunity to ask this young woman if she had considered trying to date outside her race, but it was obvious from student comments as they were leaving that the young woman had touched on a sensitive issue. Many black women on predominantly white college campuses have a difficult time finding suitable dating partners.

This is not a new issue for black women. Magazine articles from as early as the 1960s and 1970s addressed this issue from a variety of perspectives. However, few articles suggested broadening one's dating pool to include non-African American men as a possible solution. Perhaps the politics of the time (Black Power Movement, Civil Rights Movement, Women's Movement) didn't support dating interracially, but decades have passed since then, and the numerical disparity between black males and black females continues to grow, making dating outside of their race a viable option for African American women who want to get married.

There are several reasons why young black women have been reluctant to seek dating partners outside of their race. Among these reasons are the following: 1) never considered the idea due to family disapproval; 2) never considered that any man other than a black man could be attracted *to* them or *by* them; 3) fear of the unknown; 4) hair issues; and 5) low self-esteem. All of these reasons are explored in the following narratives.

Further, at another seminar on a predominantly white college campus, I was the invited speaker for a black women's group. Since few of them were dating, the young women wanted to hear more about my research on interracial dating and marriage. They were looking for suggestions on how to expand their social lives. Many of them thought it was a novel idea that someone other than a black man could be attracted *to* them or attracted *by* them and had dismissed this idea out of hand. Of those who had thought about dating interracially, some were fearful. How would they know if someone was genuinely interested in them or if they were being used as a social experiment? They were worried that they would not be accepted by a white male's friends or family, and they would incur disapproval from their black friends or family members. Some were concerned that white men or other non-African American men would never choose them over white women or other women of color. At the core of their concerns was low self-esteem, most likely a response to the relentless message American and Western societies have put forth about beauty, standards which the typical black woman can't meet. It was disturbing to hear a couple of these young black women state that even though many of the black men on campus weren't interested in them, they only had to be patient, as they believed the men would eventually return to them. I asked the young women why they would be content to be anyone's second choice and not try to find someone who would choose them first. Moreover, why would they spend their young lives alone when this need not be the case? A few of the women acknowledged that, in theory, they knew I was right, but in practice, they really didn't see how they could change the situation. I was struck by the fact that I was speaking to a group of young, attractive, intelligent college-educated black women, and many of them had never considered getting outside their comfort zone when it came to dating. Indeed, many of the young women were trapped by the view that only a black man would want them or be acceptable. If one of the reasons to attend college (and this group had knowingly enrolled at a majority white college) is to broaden one's perspective and experiences, it was interesting that when it came to dating, few considered challenging long-held beliefs about suitable partners.

While the examples detailed above are about African American women attending majority white colleges and universities, anecdotal evidence collected from black women enrolled at historically black colleges and universities indicates that this group often doesn't fare any better when it comes to dating. Once again, the numerical imbalance between black men and black women leaves many African American females without any greater prospects than their counterparts attending majority white colleges and universities.

The African American gender disparity on college campuses highlights additional issues which diminish the dating prospects for black women. Many of these issues impact all women on college campuses but are more visible among minority populations. First, large numbers of students of either sex simply aren't interested in dating or forming exclusive relationships while in college. These students may be focused on other social activities or their classes, and/or limit their social lives to going out in groups on the weekends. Students in this category may participate in casual sexual relationships, commonly known as 'hooking up', but others may not. Typical of these students is not feeling any pressure to commit or make long-term relationship choices and enjoying friendships with peers of both sexes. Second, in keeping with the idea of college providing the opportunity to explore new interests and relationships, some African American college males form interracial relationships. As one black male asked me, 'why should I limit myself exclusively to dating black women if I share interests with a white woman?' Further, he didn't understand why any black women would limit themselves to dating only black men when they might also find they had more in common with someone outside of their race.

Third, disproportionately to white homosexuals on campus, more black men are homosexual, a difference that is pronounced at many colleges and universities. Many reasons have been suggested as to why this is the case. Among these reasons, African American males who are homosexual have grown up under the limelight heterosexual black males experience in some communities, with the result that homosexuals may be more likely to complete high school and enroll in college. It is important to clarify that I am not suggesting the majority of college bound or educated black males are homosexual - only that black homosexuals tend to be more visible on a campus where there are few African American males to begin with. The end result for heterosexual African American female co-eds is simply fewer eligible black men.

The college years thus highlight the beginning of the difficulty middle class African American women face when considering prospective dating partners. Obtaining a college diploma has been a goal for middle class African Americans for generations. How ironic it is that in pursuing a college education, middle class black females may be losing out socially if they don't consider pursuing partners outside of their race to date.

The challenges black women college students face when trying to find dating partners often continue when they begin their careers. The work setting may have a broader age demographic population with fewer eligible single people.

One young black professional woman in her early 30s who grew up in a religious family and was newly engaged after several years of searching for a suitable mate poignantly described the difficulties she experienced searching for a husband within her racial/ethnic group. After becoming engaged, she wrote the following to her girlfriends on Facebook. Her emotional testimony is representative of what I have heard from other young black women about the challenges and stresses associated with dating.

> "My dearest single sisters, I want to show you my engagement photos. But look closer—I want you to see the smile that's coming from much deeper than my face; it's reflecting my soul. I wish I could give all of the ladies who are tired of waiting a glimpse into how my heart feels now. Just follow my journey for a second. My smile has always been real—it's just hidden some painful scars that I've worked really hard to allow the Lord to heal. I know the pain of loneliness, compromise, and frustration. I haven't forgotten what it feels like to wonder if my standards were too high, to question if I was looking for a man that no longer existed. I remember the Friday nights I had to figure out something to do because I promised myself I would no longer accept dates from men who were looking for a hook up, who had no intentions of committing to me—or any of the several other women they were dating simultaneously. I understand feeling unwanted and wondering if there were any black men left who still believed in marriage. I would have thrown up if one more married man propositioned me! I wanted to smack the next suitor to tell me that I'm the perfect prototype for a wife; they just weren't ready to settle down. I know the anger I had to work through with God because I followed all the rules, I waited until I was married, I married a Christian, etc.—yet my

entire world crumbled miserably and there was absolutely nothing I could do to fix it. I know the agony
of coming to terms with the reality of accepting that
the man you've given your heart to just doesn't want
you. BUT...I knew I was called to be a wife. I knew
God hadn't forgotten me, even when I felt hopeless.
I knew I was better than settling. I didn't know how
long it would take, but I was determined to encour-
age myself and change the words I spoke about my
future and the love that God promised me. And then
literally, out of nowhere, Keith came and changed my
world. Ladies, the way he loves me, pursues me, prays
for me, talks to me, laughs with me, learns with me,
encourages me, supports me... I promise you he was
worth the wait!! I would go through it all again if it
would bring me back to him. My sisters, don't settle.
Wait. It feels like absolute HELL during the process,
but you're prolonging what God is trying to do for you
by holding onto counterfeits. Be brave enough to be
alone. Work on yourself. Love yourself. He's out there
looking for you—be ready when he finds you! I'm not
brand new because now I have a man. I know the gray
area all too well. Trust me, I've played myself and I've
been played more than I care to admit. I'm just being
brave enough to share my battle wounds so you can
skip some painful steps and prepare for the right one.
The one who deserves your love. There are no shortcuts. Do the work. Honor God with your dating decisions. I don't know when, my sister, but your turn will

come. Fix your crown—you're a daughter of the most High God."(6)

Since this young woman wanted to marry within her racial/ethnic group, this requirement contributed to her dating struggles. However, again her experiences are not unique to black women. The numerical imbalance between black women and black men made her struggles more acute. Her story describes the despair and sense of hopelessness many women feel by the time they reach their early 30s and are still single when they would prefer to be married. While not specifically mentioned in her narrative, the writer undoubtedly wants to find a husband while she is still in her childbearing years. This is the real problem many women face, particularly those from families who discourage them from becoming pregnant without being married. Having children without being married is still stigmatized in many families, and this may be pronounced if the young woman is raised in a religious family.

Interviews with black women in their forties and fifties indicate that dating challenges continue throughout the life cycle, as the following narratives illustrate:

A divorced black woman in her 40s had this to say about dating: "I did not experience any dating challenges until I entered my 40s. I am very outgoing and easy on the eyes. What I discovered as I have gotten older is that the innocence and naïveté of dating decades ago is long gone. There is more deceit and contamination in the dating pool than there was before. At my age women expect a certain level of career success and 'swag' from a mate: a level of polish and business acumen. Some of us want a man that is 'suited and booted' and has a matching six-figure income. Others are not as regimented in their thinking; they look more closely at the man's character versus his bank account and educational achievements. Men are often intimidated by women who earn more than they do and thus feel they aren't needed or necessary in the relationship; they feel the women can do without them. In my mind, what is most needed is someone who can support me mentally, spiritually, emotionally, and physically—not so much his bank account. What I really want from a mate is priceless. Increasingly, I have to deal with problems and drama, including ex-wives, one, two or three; baby mamas, debt, and bankruptcy. So dating is definitely not as much fun no matter if you date within your race or interracially." (7)

Black women who are divorced with children face a different set of challenges. For example, a divorced black woman in her late forties with an eight-year-old son described her dating challenges as either easier or more difficult, depending on how one looked at it. On the one hand, when she was in her 30s and early 40s, the clock was ticking and every man she dated she looked at as a potential husband. Now, knowing that she's not going to have any more children and not going to expose her son to just anyone, dating is far less stressful. She noted that she doesn't have the pressure of thinking, "Could this be the one?" Further, she is not certain she wants to get married again (although she is open to the idea). She acknowledged that if she did decide she would like to get married again, her options are much more limited. (8)

In conversation with a fifty-year-old never married black woman about the dating challenges her generation faced as younger women, she offered several insights. She began by noting that when she was in college she didn't feel as if there were fewer black men. For one thing, at the predominantly white university she attended, she felt the black students tended to band together and support each other. Further, unlike today, even the black male athletes hung out with the black women and there was little, if any, interracial dating. Second, she was quick to point out that for her generation, if you could get admitted and receive financial aid to attend a prestigious university, your focus was not on finding a husband or wife, but totally on maximizing the college years to position yourself for a good, high-paying career. Moreover, she recalled that for the black men in particular, "they weren't just driven to get a good job in corporate America or in other professions, they wanted to be at the top in whatever field they went into…they wanted to become leaders." Third, she enjoyed her social life because she joined a sorority, Alpha Kappa Alpha Sorority Incorporated, and the black Greeks used to attend not only each other's functions on campus, but also, they attended social events with black Greeks on other campuses or in the neighboring city. There were opportunities for non-Greeks to participate in the social scene, too. Once she graduated, her social life continued to revolve around black Greek culture through alumni chapters. Fourth, she observed that there is one significant difference between how white and black women view dating. Her white women friends were far more concerned about their fertility, "their biological clock running out before they found someone to marry and have children. The black women I knew seemed to push this issue to the back of their minds…first get educated, establish yourself in a good career, and then once that was going well, think about the next step. In terms of age, this meant that the black women I knew really didn't start to get married until the middle 30s." The white women started marrying in their late 20s. Fifth, she pointed out, "Most black people have some sort of Christian religious background or orientation. For middle class African Americans, there is still a stigma attached to having children without being married. This did lead to some frustration and sadness when these women weren't able to find husbands sometime during their 30s, but most of my friends did eventually get married, with some having children well into their 40s or adopting children. I can't say I knew any black women who thought about trying to find men outside of their race; there just wasn't that mindset. By the time some women realized they wanted to get married, they were in their early 30s and guess what, now they were competing with younger women. With fewer black men to go around as you age, because many of the good ones were already married, here is where the problem arose for the black woman who wanted to get married." (9)

Another black woman observed that she first got married when she was twenty-three years old but the marriage ended in divorce after a few years because she didn't understand what it meant to be a wife or a helpmate. "I didn't realize I should be my husband's best friend. My 30s were probably the best dating decade of my life. I had the maturity I needed to date men from any racial group. In my 40s, it became very competitive in terms of dating. Your biological clock is running out and there is always this sense of rushing, trying to find someone to marry so you can have children. The 50s are the invisible decade; men don't see you anymore. A man in his fifties is looking for a 40-year-old woman; a 40-year-old man is looking for a 30-year-old woman with whom to have children. I have always worked in corporate America with younger white women, where I learned that they operate from a different dating playbook. The younger white women I work with have a plan—first, live in the city where they can socialize and meet eligible men; second, work their mid-level type jobs in corporate America; third, once settled in a career, get married and move to the suburbs. Many of them even know how many children they want to have. For black women, it is totally different. We start out with getting a good education first, then try to get good jobs. However, my experience has been that black women don't start out, despite often being more educated than many of their white counterparts, with the same salary scale as white women. We get to their salary scale about ten years later, thus putting black women behind in the dating and marriage game because we have a longer time to wait before we can afford to get married and have children. Consequently, for many black women it winds up being too late in terms of finding a partner and having children.

"In your 50s if you want to get married to a black man and you have climbed up the corporate salary scale, I have found it is like looking for a needle in a haystack, given the fact that there are far more black women than black men employed at higher levels and we have more advanced degrees, too.

"When I married my second husband, I learned that he wanted to have it both ways. He had a MBA and a PhD and while he was glad I was also educated and felt we were 'evenly yoked' in the Biblical sense, in reality, he still wanted me to be in a secondary position in the marriage, despite the fact that I earned as much as he did.

"Now that we are in the age of online dating, when I first began searching for eligible men four years ago, I found several men I could have been interested in dating. However, online dating has become like a candy store for men. Even if their profile indicates that they want to find someone, settle down and get married, the statistics demonstrate that this rarely happens. Many are always looking online for the next conquest.

"At this stage in life, I have formed a sisterhood with my 'besties'—other black women who are single—and I do things with them that I would have preferred to do with a man, including dining out and traveling. For instance, I am getting ready to travel to southern France with one of my girlfriends.

"Today, there are two sets of single black women. One set will say, 'I don't need a man; I am perfectly happy by myself.' The second set is where I fit in—women who still hope to find someone. I will keep hope alive that there is still someone out there for me, whether it happens or not. I make it my second job to try and find someone." (10)

The fundamental conundrum—how to find a suitable husband while in the childbearing years—may be particularly challenging for black women, as they tend to marry later than their white counterparts. For some women, having followed parental rules, graduating from college or obtaining advanced degrees, beginning their careers, and thinking about having children, the middle 20s to middle 30s are a sobering and stressful time. They come up against what sociologist Robert Staples discovered in the 1970s—that for every 100 college-educated black women, there are far fewer similarly educated black men (11). When you factor in men who are not interested in getting married, who date and marry outside of their race, or who are homosexual, the number of eligible black men drops dramatically. The result of this situation is exactly what I discovered when I observed the dating and marriage outcomes for a group of young middle class black people who grew up in Chicago's North Shore suburbs. The African American women wound up marrying later than the black men, often marrying men who did not have the resources or skills they had, and in some cases marrying men who had been in previous relationships and already had children. To be sure, many of these marriages may work out fine; however, there is no denying that some of these African American wives settled for marriage to black men who were not their social equals.

CHAPTER 2

HOW AND WHERE INTERRACIAL COUPLES MEET

Two questions I am often asked are how and where interracial couples meet.

If they don't meet on college campuses, there are at least five settings in which the couples I interviewed for this book, as well as for my first book, *Interracial Marriages Between Black Women and White Men* (Cambria Press; December 2008), have met. The five sites are the workplace, the military, church, the Internet, or through friends.

THE WORKPLACE

Beginning with the workplace, as increasing numbers of blacks and whites work in close proximity to each other, opportunities for interracial relationships abound. These interracial relationships form at all levels in the workplace hierarchy, but in my research, I discovered that the likelihood of developing intimate personal relationships increased at higher skill levels. Succinctly, people working on assembly lines might not have the opportunity to get to know each other as well as people working under less regulated conditions. Additionally, my prior research on interracially married couples suggested that many of them shared the same profession, including teachers, musicians, attorneys, actors, writers, and psychologists.

One problem with forming relationships at work is that there are companies or other professional groups which discourage or prohibit romantic relationships between coworkers. If two coworkers pursue a romantic relationship, one of them may be asked to leave the company or be switched to another position within the work setting. Undoubtedly these policies are in place to ensure an equitable working environment.

Even in companies where there are no policies against dating coworkers, some employees may not be interested in mixing their work relationships with romantic ones. One black woman interviewed for this book indicated that as a professional she had strict standards against dating a colleague, as she felt doing so would detract from her effectiveness in her position. Her husband went to great lengths to convince her that he was sincerely interested in her and would be discreet about their romantic relationship while at work. Even so, this woman described taking their relationship very slowly at first because if it didn't work out, she would still be expected to work with him.

THE MILITARY

The military has a long history of being a setting where interracial couples meet. Undoubtedly the close proximity under which servicemen and women interact and the dangerous conditions in which many live and work around the world heighten their sense of community. Social barriers which may be in force back home diminish when one's life is on the line. The result is the forming of relationships, including interracial ones, which endure when military service ends.

THE CHURCH

Despite the fact that the majority of churches in America are racially/ethnically segregated, several interracial couples have met at church. Many churches have sponsored events for singles, and it is through participating in these activities that some couples have met. Moreover, in some integrated communities, churches have outreached to a more diverse population in an attempt to be more inclusive, with the result that more interracial dating occurs.

Historically, some religious doctrines opposed interracial marriages, but one notable exception is the Baha'i faith. Introduced in the United States in 1893, this Middle Eastern religion promotes interracial marriage as a prerequisite to achieving world peace. There is only one Baha'i temple per continent; in the United States the Baha'i temple is located in a northern Chicago suburb, Wilmette, Illinois.

I interviewed two interracial couples who were members of the Baha'i faith for my first book on black-white marriages. As practicing Baha'is, their parents had to consent to their marriage before it could take place. If a parent refused consent for any reason, the marriage would not be allowed. How fortunate it was for these two couples that their parents supported their marriage, welcoming a new in-law from another racial/ethnic background into their family. Parental acceptance of a new family member is not assured in any marriage, so it was refreshing to learn there is a religion that reduces this uncertainty from the very beginning of the marriage relationship.

THE INTERNET

The Internet and the ever-growing number of online dating sites have provided an important opportunity for some interracial relationships to form. Increasing numbers of people from all racial/ethnic groups have met online. Online dating sites cater to a wide range of tastes, from sites designed to allow people from the same racial/ethnic groups to meet through sites designed for people who wish to date someone from their same religious or age background.

For African American women, meeting men online is problematic. Research has demonstrated that black women are the *least likely* to be selected online for dates by men of any racial/ethnic group (12), reinforcing the fact that African American women are considered the least desirable of romantic partners. However, for this study, I interviewed four black women who met their future white husbands online, including one woman whose husband deliberately sought to find African American women to date by joining a 'blacks only' dating site. In this case, the white husband indicated that he had long been attracted to black women but didn't have direct access to meeting any. Hence, he decided to go 'undercover', and his future wife didn't know he was white until he showed up for their first date. Needless to say, 'he had some explaining to do' and his future wife would not consent to dating him until he demonstrated his sincerity by continuing to pursue her.

MEETING THROUGH FRIENDS

Finally, a few interracial couples have met through mutual friends. A couple of examples from my research are illustrative of this meeting method. One black woman had a white college roommate who became one of her best friends. Even though the two women were in separate social groups due to their different academic interests, the white roommate had a white male friend she thought would be perfect for her black roommate. Turns out she was right and this couple met and eventually married. Second, one black woman had a white male friend she thought should meet her black girlfriend. Once again, this couple eventually married, too. What is striking about both these examples is that they demonstrate how some social boundaries surrounding interracial relationships have begun to abate. As recently as twenty years ago, it would have been unlikely that a white person would intentionally introduce a black person to someone white as a potential dating partner and the reverse scenario would have been equally improbable. Indeed, in the introduction, I noted it was during the beginning of the dating years that friendships between some black and white women diminished as each sought to form intimate relationships with males within their own racial/ ethnic group. When race/ethnicity ceases to be a social boundary people use when introducing potential dating partners to each other, America will have reached a significant milestone in racial harmony.

CHAPTER 3

HOW THE INTERVIEWEES WERE SELECTED FOR THIS BOOK

Twelve years ago, I interviewed fifty black-white interracially married couples for my academic study on interracial marriage. Twenty black men with white wives and thirty black women with white husbands agreed to personal in-depth interviews on their relationships. The results of this comparative research are contained in my book, *Interracial Marriages Between Black Women and White Men* (Cambria Press: December 2008). The couples who participated in this study resided primarily in the Chicago metropolitan area.

The results from this study piqued my continuing interest in the topic, particularly the marriage relationships between black women with white husbands. While the ratio of black men married to white women compared to black women married to white men is approximately 3.75:1 (13), I was interested in learning more about black women married to white men precisely because it was the *least* common of the two interracial marriage pairings. Moreover, the numerical imbalance between black women and black men presents unique dating and marriage challenges for African American women. I believe if white women experienced the degree of numerical imbalance to white men that African American women experience to black men this problem would have been addressed in the public domain and strategies to support a more numerically balanced society would have been put forth. Historically, the last time American white women experienced being in the overwhelming majority was during World War II, when over 405,000 Americans, primarily white men, lost their lives. Countless numbers of white women lost husbands and fiancés, and many of these women never married or re-married. Today women of all racial/ethnic groups outnumber men, but the societal consequences are most pronounced for black women, who have largely suffered in silence.

In seeking African American women to interview for this book, I first sent an email to black women graduate students enrolled at two universities within the Chicago area asking if any of them met the demographics of my research questions. Of the one hundred and twenty-five women I emailed, approximately 35% of the respondents fit into one or more of the three categories (i.e., dating, married to, or divorced from a white man) or knew someone they could refer me to who did. The young women in this group were between the ages of 21-35.

Second, since the publication of my first book, I had been keeping a list of new couples I would approach when I wanted to update my research. The new couples were exclusively black women married to white men and this group ranged in age from their early 30s through age 55.

Third, I have included in this book the perspectives of interracially dating or married African American women between the ages of 50-70, to give historical context to this topic.

Finally, I interviewed five white men who are involved in romantic relationships with black women. I felt it was essential to learn directly from these men why they chose black women as dating or marriage partners. American history is filled with tales of illicit relationships between black women and white men. I wanted to give voice to the current generation of white men who pursue relationships with African American women. In total, I interviewed approximately 120 people for this book and present narratives which were representative of a common pattern or singularly unique. Taken together, the reader will have a broad understanding of the challenges and rewards black women and white men face in forming romantic relationships.

CHAPTER 4

IN THEIR OWN WORDS:
AFRICAN AMERICAN WOMEN
ON DATING WHITE MEN

When it comes to dating across racial/ethnic lines, two personality traits stood out among all of the black women who participated in my study: they were confident and had high self-esteem. Many had outgoing personalities; others were more reticent, but all of them exhibited a strong and positive sense of self. Undoubtedly these personality traits would make any individual attractive to another, but still, I was delighted to learn that the black women I interviewed felt good about themselves.

Second, these women were not constrained by racial stereotypes in selecting dating partners. While all of them were well aware of the stereotypes about black women and knew the history of how some of them were treated at the hands of some white men, these factors did not impede them from dating outside their race.

Third, the women identified as African American or biracial and physically appeared as such. None of them would have been mistaken for being from another racial/ethnic group. Moreover, several of the women tended to be 'Afro-centric' in some manner, such as hairstyle choices, clothing styles or home decorations. This is an important factor to note, as one prevailing stereotype about black women who date outside their race is that they could 'pass' as white or from another minority ethnic group.

I began by asking each of the interviewees how they came to date outside their race. A common theme among most of these women was that their formative years were either spent in integrated or majority white communities. Moreover, most of these communities were comprised of middle to upper middle class people. Socializing with whites in school, sports or other community activities was a fairly normal occurrence in their lives. Only a couple of the women had grown up in a primarily African American community. No matter where these young women had grown up, the social contact they had with white people generally and white males in particular had been positive or, at a minimum, neutral, so they weren't deterred from socially interacting with them. Additionally, some of the women noted that the black males they did meet either weren't interested in them or vice versa, leaving them with little choice but to seek dates outside their race. Following are eleven narratives which are representative of the black women I interviewed who date white men.

CATHY

Cathy stated that when she was growing up, she lived in a mostly white town, and the small number of black people who attended her high school generally weren't from the same social class she was, nor were they in the honors track classes in which she was enrolled. Cathy laughed when she said that there was only one other black girl in the honors track, and no black males, so she didn't get to know any of them. Her first boyfriends wound up being young men who attended the same church she did. She dated a Puerto Rican guy and then an African American; in both cases these young men were childhood friends, and she didn't form any lasting romantic attachment to either of them. However, when she went to college, she had her first serious romantic relationship, and this was with a white guy. He was in many of the same classes, and their paths crossed frequently at campus events. They eventually started speaking when they would run into each other, and from these initial short conversations, longer ones followed. They became comfortable enough with each other that if they showed up in the cafeteria at the same time, they would often eat together. Cathy described their early relationship as "a friendship, nothing more than that." Cathy noted that at the predominantly white university she attended, she had difficulty forming similar friendships with the other African American students because 'she didn't talk like them.' She was told that she 'talked too white' and discovered also she had been socialized differently from most of the other black students. "So trying to like go and hang out with people [black] just became a big issue because it was like, 'You guys see "Wayne's World"?' And they're like, no. So they are looking at completely different movies and doing different dances and all of these things that I hadn't had any experience with." By contrast, Cathy's experience with white students was easier: "So the people I most had contact with were white students because we all had the same upbringing, same class background, same socialization in terms of music that we liked; like I'm really into alternative music."

Cathy acknowledged that she did receive some interest from black guys while in college, but they never asked her out on a date. The only males who asked her out were the white guys. "So I just went out with who asked me out because I am traditional enough to not ask a guy out first." The one black boyfriend she had in college was nice, but that was it. When she started working, she traveled frequently for her job, primarily meeting people who were either South Asians or whites. The males would invite her to go out with them or join them for dinner. The men weren't boyfriends but they made her feel included and thus enhanced her comfort level dating outside her race. As Cathy's career progressed, she met few black male colleagues, and none were interested in her. She did, however, meet several white male colleagues who asked her out. Over time, she recognized that white males were more likely than black men to demonstrate interest in her.

I asked Cathy how her parents felt about her primarily dating white men. She responded that her family didn't care. When I asked if she had met any of the parents of the white men she dated and if the family accepted her, Cathy said that she had met many of the parents, and generally she felt welcomed by them. However, she noted, that a couple of the men had parents who she thought accepted her because they knew the community and neighborhood in which she had grown up and recognized she must have come from the same social class, making it easier to accept her. She acknowledged that there were a couple of white parents who didn't accept her, or if they did, other family members didn't. In the latter situation, lack of parental acceptance doomed the relationship since Cathy wasn't about to deal with any family tension over race. As she noted, "Life is too short and there are too many other people I can date to spend time worrying about dealing with someone whose family has these types of issues."

JANE

Jane offered another perspective on how she began dating white men. Originally from the East Coast, when her parents decided to move to the Chicago area, their first consideration was where her brother and she would attend school. Paramount for her father, especially, was that they attend schools in a community where it was expected all of the students would enroll in four-year colleges. This led her parents to buy a home in a fairly affluent northern Chicago suburb. Jane noted that there were only a couple of other black families in the neighborhood, along with a few Asian families. The majority of families were white, which was reflected in the school system.

Jane was very athletic when she was in junior high school and as a result belonged to several sports teams. Her primary acquaintances and friends were white, but she did meet a few other minority students when any of her teams traveled. Overall though, she lived in a white world and only interacted with black people when she attended family reunions or other gatherings. She indicated that she didn't think much about race growing up because living where she did, race didn't come up as an issue in her interactions with whites. With her extensive participation in sports, her family was relatively well known since they attended her games. She was fairly popular in school and described herself as a 'late bloomer' when it came to dating. During her senior year in high school, Jane was surprised when she was voted to be in the homecoming court, which meant she had to attend the prom. She went to the prom with a longtime friend, a white male who was also very athletic.

When Jane enrolled in college in Chicago, she expanded her friend network and began dating more seriously. Her first college boyfriend was black, followed by an Asian boyfriend, another black boyfriend and then she met her husband (Tom), who is white. Jane remarked that she was open to dating people from a variety of backgrounds because she hadn't dated much before college and wanted to make up for lost time. She had a serious relationship with her second black boyfriend and she did consider race when they broke up and she started dating her husband. She wondered for the first time if race was going to be an issue in the relationship. She was introduced to Tom through her Asian roommate. Tom and her roommate were in many of the same classes, and one day walking through campus, she came upon the two of them leaving class. While she was talking to them, a friend of Tom's joined the group. The four of them decided to go out to dinner and from this event, Jane states that she was the one to initiate the relationship. Sometime after the dinner, she called Tom to see if he was interested in getting together again because she found him to be very interesting. This was around Valentine's Day and she asked him if he had other plans. When Tom responded no, she suggested they get together for a movie, which they did. After asking Tom if he wanted to go out again, she began to get a little apprehensive because she had become more attuned to racial issues around dating since being in college. However, she soon learned Tom had grown up in a very integrated suburb and that his high school girlfriend had been black. Moreover, Jane became impressed with how savvy Tom was, noting that he was far savvier about issues surrounding race, gender and relationships than she was. Tom had grown up with and had close friendships with both black and white males, which made the relationship easier for Jane. She didn't feel as if she had to explain her background to him.

Jane and Tom continued to date throughout college but then the stress of trying to figure out their next career steps took a toll on their relationship. They had an on-again, off-again relationship for several years, but never completely broke up. When Jane completed her PhD and decided to take a post-doc opportunity in the South, Tom volunteered to move with her since he didn't like the idea of her being alone in a new city. Jane was impressed that Tom would give up his position in Chicago just to be with her in a new environment. As Jane said, "It wasn't like I was going to Los Angeles or New York; I was going to Memphis, a very conservative city," and she did have concerns about how an interracial couple would fare there. When Tom's employer agreed to allow him to continue his position working remotely, their decision was confirmed. For three years, Jane and Tom lived in the South.

I asked Jane if Tom and she had encountered any difficulties as an interracial couple in the South. She responded that overall their lives were pretty similar to the lives they led in Chicago, but there were several small incidents which had racial overtones. Jane attributed these micro-aggressions to the fact that she was accustomed to a greater racial mix in Chicago and there wasn't much diversity in the southern city in which they resided. The three years Tom and Jane spent living together solidified their desire to get married, which they did in a small ceremony, with just their immediate families and close friends present. Jane noted that by the time Tom and she married, they had known each other for nearly a decade.

TERESA

Teresa is twenty-seven years old and as she pointed out in her interview, tall for a woman—nearly six feet. She thought that her height was a problem when it came to dating black men because some of those she knew were not as tall as she is, and as a result were not attracted to her. She discovered that the white men she met didn't seem to be concerned about her height, and of the four white males she dated, two were shorter than her. Teresa grew up in a predominantly black community but went to integrated schools. Early in her education, she discovered she enjoyed science classes more than other subjects, eventually majoring in chemistry in college and pursuing a PhD in the field. She believes her interest in science and chemistry, which mostly attracted white or Asian students, accounts for why she wound up dating outside her race. Often she wound up paired with whites or Asians when working on experiments and would socialize with them outside of class or labs. Moreover, she enjoys going to the theatre and knows many acting students. Between her two interests, she has a strong network of mostly white friends.

Teresa is in the fairly unique position of having met her white boyfriends through her white girlfriends. She has had a couple of white women as roommates and both of them introduced her to white men. In fact, she noted that neither of her roommates thought too much about race when suggesting she meet someone they knew. Teresa felt it was their perception that she would have a lot in common with a few of the white men they knew.

Over the past seven years, Teresa has dated four men: three whites and one African American. Only one of the men is in graduate school; two were already working, one as a graphic designer, and one owned a printing business. The African American boyfriend had started college, but switched majors a few times and as of our interview had not finished yet. Teresa didn't feel that his lack of finishing college was a major problem in the relationship; the physical distance between them was more of an issue. During the three years they were together, he moved out of the area, resulting in their having a long distance relationship, which didn't work well.

The three white men Teresa dated, including her current boyfriend, have all been relationships which lasted a year or more. She indicated that the reasons two of the relationships ended had nothing to do with racial issues. In one case, after a few months, they simply no longer got along; in the second case, he wanted her to move with him to another city and she wanted to stay in the Chicago area. In an interesting twist, one of her former white boyfriends had grown up in Oak Park, Illinois (a racially integrated Chicago suburb), and his parents were divorced. His father remarried an African American woman so he had a black stepmother to whom he was close. However, the relationship with Teresa ended because he didn't feel ready to emotionally commit to any woman at that time in his life. After they had been broken up for about six months, she ran into him again and he wanted to resume casually dating. Teresa indicated that she didn't want to be in limbo again in the relationship but against her better judgment agreed to go out with him. After a few more months of dating, she realized the relationship was not progressing to another level so she ended it for good. Teresa contended that this boyfriend probably felt comfortable dating black women because of his stepmother.

Teresa has been with her current boyfriend for about eighteen months and thus far feels this is the most comfortable and stable of her relationships. Her current boyfriend is from Texas and his parents divorced when he was young. His mother and stepfather live in a neighborhood which now makes him uncomfortable because it is not integrated. He has become more aware of racial issues and at times Teresa feels he is overly sensitive to how she might be feeling about going out with him. For example, he gets concerned about the depictions of African Americans in movies and doesn't want to go to any movies which could be offensive to her. She will tell him, "It's just a movie" but he is still very aware of her feelings. Teresa does feel though that his heightened racial sensitivity indicates the depth of his feelings for her.

In terms of sexual intimacy, Teresa indicated that all but one of the relationships was intimate. She prefaced her remarks by noting that she grew up Catholic and her father was a very strong influence in her life. He taught her to be wary of a man's intentions and not to trust any man too soon. As Teresa put it, "My father wanted to make certain that I wasn't just a quick booty call." Teresa stated that as a result, she doesn't engage in sex early in any relationship. I asked if she felt more comfortable having sex with her black boyfriend than any of her white boyfriends and she responded, "No, race isn't on my mind if the relationship is about to become sexual; only if I really trust the guy."

ELISE

Elise is a 40-year-old divorcee who works in corporate America by day to allow her to pursue her true passion, acting. She grew up in a poor, predominantly black neighborhood in Detroit, went to college in the Chicago area, and then began to move around the country. She was married to a black man for three years, and after the marriage ended she became more open to dating outside her race because she wasn't meeting many other black men. Being in the theatre world, she met many white men and a couple of Latino men. While none of these early post-divorce relationships were serious, still they allowed her to form friendships for the first time with white and Latino men.

She became attracted to one white actor and in hindsight, thinks she was attracted to his acting ability. They began a flirtation; turned out he was attracted to her, too. As they got to know each other, they discovered they were the first person of another race that either had dated. This bond—being each other's first interracial relationship—meant that they developed a very close friendship. They dated each other exclusively for two and a half years, which Elise said was a long time for her. After all, she had only been married for three years.

The relationship ended on friendly terms, the same as with her husband. She hadn't dated much since. She attributed this to just not meeting anyone else yet. She occasionally checks free online dating sites, but is not interested in paying to meet new men. Fortunately for Elise, she has men who serve as companions, even if not romantic partners, so she doesn't feel lonely or in any rush to get married again. While she would prefer to find another black man, she is definitely not against dating again outside her race. The main reason she would like to marry a black man is because she feels it would be easier to share life with someone from the same racial/ethnic background. On the other hand, she recalled how hard she had to work when she was married in order to help her husband pay child support for his two daughters. It was not until many years after her divorce that she realized how much debt her husband had, and how much she struggled to help him. She would not be interested in getting married again to anyone who had that much debt.

When I asked Elise if she noticed any differences between dating black men and white men, she responded, "Yes, respect." With her white boyfriend, she always felt he had a level of respect for her that was missing in her relationship with her black husband. Another word she used to describe her white boyfriend was 'gentle.' She felt he had "a true kind of fundamental, like care—I'm going to look out for you and take care of you." When she shared this sentiment with her father, who was dating a white woman at the time, he completely agreed with Elise's assessment. He thought that white women possessed this same quality of gentleness in their demeanor, too.

I asked Elise if she had met any of her white boyfriend's family and how they treated her. She responded that she had met his parents and grandfather. She got along well with his mother, in particular. She felt his grandfather was not initially happy about their relationship, but over time found himself liking her and enjoying their conversations. While she doesn't think she changed him completely, she felt he did come to accept her.

Elise's parents didn't have any problems with her interracial relationship. From the time she was a child, her mother discouraged her from describing people in racial terms. For example, when she met new girls and would tell her mother that she met a 'white girl', her mother would ask her why the girl's race was important. Her mother made her think about why she thought it was necessary to identify someone by race. After her parents divorced, her father dated both black and white women.

The primary reason Elise's interracial relationship ended was because her boyfriend was a recovering alcoholic. She noted, however, that even when drinking, he was never physically or verbally abusive to her. She also noted that she was not the first in her family to date interracially. She has a niece and a nephew who both dated and married whites. There were other family members married to whites, too. One of her uncles even made a joke about it, wondering why so many family members were marrying outside their race.

MELISSA

Melissa is a thirty-year-old woman who recently completed her PhD in biology. She is working on her medical school degree. She grew up in a middle class black family and has lived in several cities across the country due to her father's job. Both of her parents are professionals. When she moved to the Chicago area, she lived close to a church which was known for its outreach to younger people. This church had several programs for singles and one day she decided to check it out. Melissa had been raised in a Christian church primarily comprised of African Americans and was pleasantly surprised when she visited this new church to see how diverse the congregation was. While attending one of the programs for singles, she met her current white boyfriend, John.

Prior to John, she had dated two other white men, but neither of these relationships were long term. The first lasted about three months and ended because she felt he was a sex addict and not interested in anything more in the relationship. The second relationship lasted approximately six months and ended because he was under-employed and stressed about obtaining a teaching position. After the second relationship ended, she had begun to think she should try to find a black boyfriend so she wouldn't have "that extra layer of race to deal with." So when she met John, she wasn't thinking of him as a romantic prospect, and moreover, initially she was a bit put off by him.

I asked Melissa to explain what she meant by 'the extra layer of race' in her relationships and if she had experienced any negative social experiences while dating white men. She promptly responded that she had experienced numerous negative interactions from white waitresses when with her second white boyfriend. Melissa described this boyfriend as being very cute and tall, with dark hair and blue eyes. Once while they were sitting at a restaurant bar, the waitress came over to ask for his drink order while ignoring her. When he told the waitress that the two of them were together, she still only made eye contact with him. It was as if she couldn't accept that they were a couple. Melissa went on to say that she caught random people looking occasionally at her when the two of them were walking on the street. She noted in particular the looks from older black men.

It was during Melissa's second relationship that she began to think about how race impacts interracial couples. While watching a documentary on interracial children in Britain, the commentator referred to these children as 'tinted' and she began to wonder how her boyfriend's parents were going to feel if they had 'tinted' grandchildren. She admitted though that she had met her second boyfriend's parents and they seemed to be okay with her. Her own parents were okay with the relationship, too, although her mother had some reservations. Her mother is skeptical about 'baggage' she believes a white man is going to have when dating a black woman. She worries that one day Melissa's boyfriend will 'wake up' and want to return to a relationship with a white woman if for nothing other than the reason that it will be easier to deal with socially.

Fortunately for Melissa, in her current relationship with John, she feels he understands even better than she does the baggage he is acquiring due to his relationship with her. John told her he knows he is going to be treated differently by extended family members and perhaps even in the work setting. She noted that often there is a subtle shift in how bosses and coworkers treat a white man with a black wife. Melissa described this shift this way:

"…I'm trying to think how to describe it. I don't know if it's like a holdover from the time when they [white people] used the word 'nigger-lover', you know, that idea. But it's just— you're a white male, and that carries with it a certain amount of privilege in society, obviously, and so you are willingly attaching yourself within marriage to a black woman. It's like, well, what does that say about you as a white man? It's just like a shift in the way that they're [white men] approached, treated, and dealt with; opportunities in some cases that are offered. So it's like in some ways, their [white males] social stature kind of comes down." Melissa went on to state that times are much better today for white men with black wives, but her perception is still true.

Returning to the subject of why Melissa was initially turned off to John, she said at first he came on too strong. He had a swagger about him that was off-putting. Furthermore, she thought he was interested in her friend. However, as they got to know each other better through the church program, she came to realize what a good person he was. He emailed her one day to let her know that he would like to get to know her better outside of church, which she found endearing—that he took the time to write down his feelings. Being flattered at how openly he pursued her, she decided there was no reason not to give the relationship a chance.

Melissa was quick to note that she doesn't specifically choose white men but goes out with those men who pursue her. She doesn't believe dating outside their race will be the salvation for every black woman but thinks that people know in their hearts who is right for them. She is grateful that she has John in her life because even if he is white, she feels 'he gets it' in terms of racial issues, thereby strengthening their relationship.

MARSHA

Marsha is a 23-year-old black woman who grew up in a small all black community in the South with her mother, brother and grandfather. Her father was not in her life until she went to college. She describes her community as working class, one she knew she would be leaving after she graduated from high school. At twenty-three, she was already in graduate school, having skipped a couple of grades and determined to do well. When I asked her to describe her dating life, she told me that in high school she had experienced a few dates with black guys, but it was not until she was in college at a prestigious Catholic school that she started dating outside her race. Her primary reason for dating outside her race in college was that there simply weren't many black men on the campus. She knew about sixty black women students in her class, but didn't think there were more than eight black male students. When I asked her why she selected a college with so few black students, she responded that the school had heavily recruited in her town and she was given a full scholarship. Moreover, despite the racial component of the university, she actually loved the place and hopes to be able to contribute to a scholarship fund there once she starts working full-time.

Marsha discussed the differences she noticed in dating Africans, Hispanics, African Americans, and whites. She noted first that the black men she dated did not want to make any commitments to her. She didn't like feeling that she was just one of the many women these men were dating. It came down to self-respect. She admitted that a few of these men were nice, but none of them wanted to define their relationship as exclusive.

Her Hispanic boyfriend was very open and willing to commit to a relationship. He even took her to meet all of his family and she felt welcomed, but the relationship ended when she left the city where she was working to move to Chicago. The African man she dated was too controlling in the relationship and she knew this would not work out long term. She likes feeling like she has some control in a romantic relationship. Finally, her best relationships have been with white men for all of the reasons the other ones didn't work out. She recalled that her white boyfriends were ready to make a commitment to the relationship even before she was, wanted to have an egalitarian relationship, and generally were more supportive of her life goals.

Additionally, none of them were threatened by her political ambitions, something she felt a couple of the other men were. Overall, she feels that she had more in common with the white men she dated.

When I asked Marsha why some of the relationships ended with the white men, she responded that primarily it was due to distance and different career goals.

I asked Marsha if she had any reservations about dating outside her race, to which she responded yes. Her reservations centered on making certain that she didn't come across as 'easy' or as 'exotic'. She purposely dressed in a conservative manner and presented herself in a professional way to discourage men from thinking she was going to fulfill any racial fantasies about black women. Moreover, she noticed that white men were more likely to approach her if her hair was straight as opposed to being in a natural style.

Marsha recalled the time when she was seated next to a white man about her age on an airplane trip who seemed very excited to talk with her. They wound up talking for the entire two-hour plane trip and he asked her for a date by the time the plane landed. She gave him her phone number and he called her right away. They dated for about four months before his job transferred him to another city.

Currently Marsha is in a fairly long-term relationship with a white boyfriend. Since they are both in graduate school, she is not certain where the relationship will go once they complete their degrees. However, she is happy with the way the relationship is progressing and feels she will know if it is meant to continue as time passes.

RENEE

Renee is twenty-nine years old and has just completed her PhD in psychology. She grew up in a poor black neighborhood on Chicago's West Side, but was fortunate that she was able to attend a magnet high school. She is the first one in her family to finish college, having attended a liberal arts school on a full scholarship. Renee knew from the time she was in high school that she wanted to become a practicing psychologist. However, she knew that in order to reach her career goal she would have to leave her neighborhood, where few people ever graduate from college.

When Renee went to college, this was the first time she lived among white people. She had known white students in high school, but counted few of them as friends. At the liberal arts college she attended, she shared a dorm room with a white roommate. This was quite the learning experience for her. She learned what 'white privilege' looks like, even though her roommate never flaunted her wealth. Renee said that "[her roommate] just took for granted she was going to finish college, and that she would have the necessary resources to do it."

Renee stated that she worked part-time throughout her college years while doing well in her classes. She didn't have as much of a social life as other students because of the demands on her time. By the time she was a college junior, she was clear about her future professional career and applied to graduate school.

In graduate school, she continued to do well but allowed herself more time to socialize. Even though she was one of few African American students in her program, she tried to be active in the black graduate student group. She also attended conferences and other psychology meetings to start the networking process for future employment. It was at one of these conferences that she met her first white boyfriend, who was also in a graduate program.

Renee describes their meeting as 'nothing out of the ordinary.' When she was presenting her research, Peter was just one of many attendees who expressed interest in it. During the conference lunch, they wound up sitting at the same table and struck up a conversation. She thought nothing of it but did tell Peter that she would be going to the graduate student mixer after the conference ended.

At the conference party, she spoke with many of the other graduate students and eventually saw Peter talking to some of his peers. When she approached him, he introduced her to his friends and proceeded to include her in their conversation. She wound up spending about thirty minutes with this group, and when she finally went to excuse herself, Peter asked her if they could stay in touch. She gave him her email address and phone number, not thinking that this exchange of information meant too much, "just his way of networking."

Within about a week of the conference, Peter emailed her and they agreed to get together again over dinner a week later. Renee remembers thinking that this turn of events was beginning to sound "like a date." Having never dated outside her race before, she did wonder how "this was going to work out" but decided to just take a wait and see attitude.

Since they were both graduate students with limited funds, Renee offered to split the cost of their dinner, but Peter insisted on paying for her. They had a good time, discussed how they got to where they were in school, and agreed to stay in touch. This was the start of their relationship.

Over the next couple of years in graduate school, Renee and Peter continued to date and provided the social support each other needed to get through their educational programs. Renee told her parents she had met someone special, and while they weren't surprised that Peter was white, "they really didn't know how to react to this…because they don't have white friends." She felt her father had the most concerns about her relationship because he "wasn't used to the idea of a white man dating me." She knew "he had a lot of preconceived notions about what kind of person Peter was." Her mother was "not exactly accepting, [that she was dating a white man] but recognized that since I had left home years ago, I probably knew what I was doing."

Renee hasn't met any of Peter's family in person because they live on the West Coast and she hasn't traveled to meet them. They do, however, know about her, and she has had several Skype conversations with his mother. Peter's parents are divorced, and he is closest to his mother and sister. Renee believes that they approve of and like her. She senses that his mother "very much respects me."

I asked Renee if other than her parents' reaction to her interracial relationship, there were any other issues related to race which concerned her. She responded by acknowledging that if Peter and she got married, they would be the first interracial couple in her family and most likely there would be some social awkwardness with other relatives and friends. Renee thought that was to be expected because her lifestyle was so different from most of her family. Peter had a couple of cousins who had married Hispanics, "so it wasn't as much of a stretch for his family." Renee acknowledged receiving 'looks' occasionally from mostly older black men when walking with Peter, but shrugged this off "as just to be expected."

Renee stated that Peter and she have discussed getting married but want to wait until they are in stable jobs. Both of them have some educational debt they want to reduce before taking on wedding costs. They moved in together about a year ago to begin saving money and would like to marry in 2018.

YOLANDA

Yolanda is in her late 50s and grew up in the Midwest in a fairly prominent political family. She is divorced from her first husband, who was African American and by whom she has two adult children. Yolanda moved to the Chicago area for her job as well as for a new start after her divorce. Living in a predominantly white suburban area, she started attending a church she had heard about with a diverse congregation and which was not too far from her home. While attending one of the church fundraisers, she met John, a divorcee with two children, just like her.

Yolanda described John as "the kind of man she didn't think still existed." When they were casually introduced, she felt an immediate attraction to him. She described him as being so easy to talk to, and his race "never really crossed my mind." She further added that they were in similar occupations and had a lot in common. As much as she enjoyed John's company, their relationship started out slowly. For one thing, she wasn't interested in getting too involved too quickly because she felt she still needed to recover from her divorce. John had been divorced for more than a decade.

Over time, Yolanda learned that John had dated a few women after his divorce, including a couple of other African American women. Yolanda teased him that "once he went black, he never went back", which was actually true. Yolanda also liked that John had taken the time before he met her to engage in counseling to help him come to terms with why his marriage ended and what he would do differently in subsequent relationships.

After dating John for about two years, the two of them moved in together. Yolanda said she wasn't interested in remarrying after her divorce, but "John was the closest I got to making another commitment."

Their relationship was going well when John was diagnosed with a terminal illness after they had been together for about eight years. During the time they had been a couple, Yolanda, too, had experienced a life threatening illness, and John had taken care of her. When he became ill, she took care of him until his death. Five years after his death, she still grieves for him even as her life and career have moved forward. She hasn't met anyone else yet and remarked that "John would be a hard act to follow."

DIANE

Diane has been dating Craig for four and a half years and recently they bought a house together. They plan on getting married in 2018. Diane is working on her Master's degree, teaching school part time and Craig is a school psychologist. They are both in their early 30s. Diane grew up in Germany but settled in Chicago after college. Craig grew up in a Chicago suburb.

Diane and Craig met at work during the last month of the school year. Craig had reason to work with a student in Diane's classroom. Every time he went to Diane's class to pick up the student, they managed to talk with each other for a few minutes. Diane admitted that she had seen Craig throughout the academic year and had developed a little crush on him. However, before he was working with one of her students, she never had the opportunity to talk with him.

Having grown up in Germany, Diane was comfortable dating whites. She said she preferred "tall, skinny white boys" in high school and Craig very much fit this profile. Had it not been near the end of the school year, they might not have gotten to know each other because Craig definitely didn't believe in mixing his personal relationships with his work relationships. Fortunately, when he met Diane in her classroom, it was within two weeks of school ending for the summer.

Both Craig and Diane enjoy riding bikes and over that summer got to know each other through this activity. Craig had recently ended another long-term relationship and wasn't thinking he would get involved again soon. Their bike riding dates were an easy way to get to know each other without any romantic commitment. At the end of one of their bike rides, they met some other friends they knew at a restaurant. Following a few drinks, Diane leaned over and gave him a kiss. Craig was so surprised at the spontaneity of this gesture that he wound up kissing her back. From that point forward, the relationship became romantic.

Diane said she was just so excited at being out with Craig after having experienced a few disappointments with men she had met through Okay Cupid (an online site) that she wanted to "have at least a good memory of kissing Craig even if the relationship didn't go anywhere." Diane had met one black man online and she thought things were going well between them when he pulled back from the relationship and she was heartbroken. A few months after Craig and she started dating, the man called her again and wanted to resume their relationship, but by that time, she was over him.

I asked Diane if she were concerned about racial issues when they started to date. Diane responded that she only thought about race when it came time to meet Craig's family. While his parents were warm and friendly right from the beginning, she initially picked up some reserve on the part of his grandparents, particularly his grandfather.

Craig's grandparents hoped to live long enough to see him get married, but being 'Old World' Italian, they thought he would be interested in someone Italian. When they discovered Diane was black, they didn't have much to say about this, and over time she believes they definitely accepted her and now even joke around with her.

Diane stated that as far as her family was concerned, her mother and grandparents liked Craig. Her father is not in her life; her parents divorced when she was quite young and her mother remarried. Diane felt that one of the most important things about being in an interracial relationship was to be true to yourself. For example, for many years she used to straighten her hair, but decided that this look was not who she was, so she wears her hair 'natural' in a short, curly style.

Her sister has a stronger black identity than she does in part because she mostly grew up in America. She is much darker skinned than Diane, and she can't imagine her dating outside her race. On the other hand, she has a cousin who is married to a Jewish guy, and Diane thinks she tries too hard to assimilate into that culture. Diane feels comfortable in both black and white cultures and thinks this is because of the different places she lived growing up as well as being more educated than her sister.

CELESTE

Celeste is twenty-nine years old and grew up in a fairly affluent family. Her father is an attorney and her mother worked part-time as a social worker. The oldest of three children, she has a Master's degree and is employed at the executive level in a large non-profit organization. She gave a little chuckle when I asked her how she came to date outside her race. She explained, "It is a good thing you are asking me this question now; had you met me a decade ago, I wouldn't have fit into this category, and truthfully, it is a little strange that I am doing so now."

Celeste explained that growing up she lived in a middle class predominantly black suburb of Chicago. Her parents were much attuned to the black community and her mother belonged to two African American social clubs. She went to an integrated public high school where she had friends who were black, white and Hispanic, but still, her closest friends were African American. She never gave it much thought that she would ever date outside her race because she knew several black males. Some of them were sons of her parents' friends and some she knew from school. When she needed a date for her senior prom, a couple of her black male friends volunteered to escort her.

Celeste attended a large Midwestern university, where she majored in psychology and participated in many campus groups, especially those organized by black students. She remarked that it was during college she realized there were fewer black men than black women. Despite this fact, she still had a good social life while in college and went out with a few of the black men, even though nothing serious ever developed. She said she didn't consider exploring dating outside her race while in college because she wasn't looking to make a lasting romantic connection during that time.

After college, Celeste returned to the Chicago area to begin working on her Master's degree. She was able to get a part-time position in her field, which put her on her current career track. When she completed her education, she was offered a full-time position with the organization.

All the while Celeste was in graduate school, she continued to exclusively date black men. She also joined a few online dating sites to broaden her dating options, but only met one black man, and while she thought he was a nice person, there was no special connection with him. This was the same way she felt about the other black men she dated. They were nice people, but there was no real spark with any of them. Celeste recounted how a few of her black girlfriends told her that she was lucky she could be so choosy, but really thought she was 'pushing her luck.' She considered her friends' advice, but said, "I can't see myself just settling for someone because I may not meet anyone else [other black men]".

One day at work, her supervisor asked her to attend a meeting comprised of people employed at similar organizations throughout the city. The group was charged with completing a joint work project. After the introductions, the group was divided up and she found herself seated next to David. Celeste didn't pay much attention to David; he didn't stand out in any way. "He was just an average looking white guy, nothing unusual."

From this first meeting, Celeste and David met again at several follow-up meetings. One of the meetings lasted past the end of the work day and the group decided to go out for drinks. When the group was seated at the restaurant, the conversation turned to their personal lives. Celeste said she became interested in David because she discovered they had mutual hobbies. He enjoyed going out to listen to jazz, dining at little-known restaurants, and exploring Chicago neighborhoods. Celeste stated that "David went from being someone I had to work with to being someone I wanted to get to know better. He was an interesting guy."

The next time the group met, Celeste said David and she had a warmer relationship. She said that the ice had been broken between them....and the whole group was more relaxed with each other. By the time the work project was completed, Celeste said most of the group agreed to stay in touch with each other. David asked Celeste if she wanted to get together for lunch or drinks again.

Celeste met David for drinks after work a week later. Drinks turned into dinner and she hated it when the evening ended. On impulse, Celeste told David that the next time they met, drinks would be on her. David responded, "When?" so they set another date for the following week. This turned out to be the beginning of their relationship.

On the second date, when David took Celeste home, she invited him inside. She was quick to note "this wasn't an invitation for sex" but she felt comfortable enough with him that she didn't want the evening to end so early [8:30 p.m.]. They listened to some jazz and started talking about how they wound up in their respective positions. They both had to work the next day so David left around 10:30 p.m.

Celeste and David continued to occasionally date even though she had another man in her life. The relationship wasn't exclusive, but she felt it was serious enough that David should know about him. The other man was African American and for the first time she thought about what he would think if he knew she was dating a white guy. In fact, "I had a reality check...what was I doing dating a white guy?"

Celeste said her African American boyfriend was someone she thought might be long term, but he was very upfront about not wanting to be in an exclusive relationship. Celeste appreciated his honesty, admitted understanding why he felt this way, but recognized that his position wasn't doing her any good. Celeste was very forthcoming when she said the matter was settled when not long after that conversation she first made love with David. "For the first time in my life, I felt like this was someone who wanted me and no one else...no strings attached. You don't know what a good feeling this is...I can stop searching. I can just relax and love him back." As of this writing, Celeste and David have been together for three years and plan to marry next year.

BRITTANY

Brittany is 40 years old and grew up as the only child in an upper middle class family in a racially diverse community. Brittany noted that due to the neighborhood in which she was raised, coupled with attending private schools, she felt more at ease among whites than she ever did with other African Americans. Her childhood friends were primarily white and many of these friendships are still ongoing. When it came time to apply to college, Brittany decided it was time to leave the nest, enrolling in a California liberal arts college. After a year in California, Brittany decided college was not for her and returned to the Midwest. She got her first real job in a neighboring state and decided to move there. She recalled that this was the first time she experienced racism, observing that a few of the white employees were not friendly, and in fact, were threatened by her. Despite not having completed college, she had acquired skills which allowed her to quickly move up the ladder in the workplace. Additionally, she was not dependent on her paycheck to support her since her parents subsidized her income, which meant she could live in a nicer area than most of her colleagues.

Brittany stated that she became interested in good health and nutrition practices, enrolling in a health club and working out three to four times weekly. Before long, she said she was in the best physical shape of her life, drawing attention from men she believes would not otherwise have ever noticed her.

About a year after her move back to the Midwest, she met Aaron at a club. Aaron was an IT technician and had grown up on a farm. Brittany laughed when she recalled telling her parents that she had met this great guy "who was a farmer." Her parents were aghast, wondering how she had managed to meet and form a romantic relationship with a young white man who came from an environment and social class totally different from theirs. Brittany believed that initially her parents were probably envisioning her future life as similar to "American Gothic" (the painting by Grant Wood). Brittany brought Aaron home one weekend to meet her parents and says that her father was non-committal, "saying only that if I was happy, then he would be happy for me." Her mother, on the other hand, was more 'measured in her response' noting that Aaron most likely would not be able to support her in the manner to which she had grown accustomed. Moreover, Aaron was helping support his mother following his father's death, and Brittany's mother wondered how the two of them (Brittany and Aaron's mother) would get along. Unspoken was the thought that while Aaron was nice, "he really wasn't good enough for me. He wasn't a professional in the traditional sense and didn't share their upwardly mobile values."

Brittany's parents, however, had long recognized it would be a 'long shot' that she would find an African American boyfriend. For one thing, they had observed that Brittany never seemed to 'click' with any of the sons of their black friends. At the private schools she attended, Brittany hadn't formed any attachments to the few other enrolled black students. As Brittany noted, "the black people I knew growing up thought I talked too white and had too many 'white interests.'"

Brittany and Aaron decided to move in together after dating for nearly a year. At the time, Brittany had decided to return to school part-time to finish her Bachelor's degree in her new field and Aaron agreed to support her. His willingness to financially support her while she went back to school made an important impression on Brittany's parents, who began to view Aaron in a more positive light. As Brittany stated, "Aaron went from not being good enough to having more substance than they thought." During this same time period, Brittany met Aaron's mother and sister. Brittany describes Aaron's mother as initially uncomfortable around her, which she attributed to not only her race, but also to her being a little intimidated by Brittany's background. As Brittany stated, "Aaron's mother didn't see many black people in rural Iowa, other than the ones she saw when she went to the shopping mall, and I didn't sound like any of them." The two women bonded over food. Aaron's mother taught Brittany and Aaron's sister how to cook several favorite recipes. When the three of them would get together, cooking was a favorite activity.

Aaron and Brittany lived together for three years while she finished her degree. During the time they lived together, Aaron kept his promise to be the breadwinner. However, once she completed college and was able to work full-time again, Aaron expected her to share household expenses.

This is when their relationship began to take a downward spiral. Brittany said that Aaron worked hard and they lived on a strict budget. He believed in living within his means; he wasn't interested in being in debt or keeping up with the Jones. Brittany acknowledged that she had grown up in a family where money was not discussed or seemed to be an issue. She had never drawn up a budget, much less felt she had to live within one. To be sure, she knew how much money she needed to meet her monthly expenses; however, if she ran short or wanted to buy something she couldn't afford, her parents would bail her out. Aaron didn't want Brittany to ask her parents for money or to remain dependent on them once she completed her degree. They had discussed getting married once she was finished with school, but when it became obvious that they had different views about money, Aaron gave her an ultimatum. He told her that she had to pay her own way and get herself out of credit card debt before he would marry her. He had grown up on a farm, where his parents taught his sister and him how to budget and the value of money at an early age. He told Brittany that if they couldn't agree on how to spend and save money, their relationship would not work long term.

Brittany stated that she tried living according to Aaron's rules for a while but felt constrained in the relationship. She didn't like being tied to a strict set of financial rules once she was back working full-time. The relationship ended two years after Brittany completed college because Aaron became frustrated that she wasn't trying hard enough to become fully financially independent of her parents. He wanted to save money for a home down payment and wound up having less to put aside because Brittany found saving and budgeting too difficult. The tension this caused in their relationship was too much of a barrier to overcome. Brittany admitted that it was difficult for her to make this kind of lifestyle adjustment being the only child of well-to-do parents. Moreover, if it weren't for Aaron's pride, most likely her parents would have given them a substantial amount of money as a down payment on a home if they had gotten married. Her parents wound up giving her a down payment on a condo after Aaron and she broke up. As of this writing, Brittany is still single and Aaron married another woman two years after their relationship ended.

SUMMARY

The eleven narratives presented in this section on black women who date white men were representative of the larger group interviewed. Being self-confident allowed these women to explore dating across the racial/ethnic divide. Most of their interracial relationship experiences were positive, even if a few of them wished they could have found personal happiness with a black man. It is important to note that these women didn't hold any preconceived expectations they would have a negative experience dating outside their race.

CHAPTER 5

BLACK WOMEN MARRIED TO WHITE MEN

The largest group of black women interviewed for this book were those who are married to white men. Included in this section are fourteen interviews which are representative of the thirty couples who participated in this section of my study. Seven women were interviewed with their husbands; seven were interviewed by themselves. Their stories highlight the rewards and challenges of being interracially married. The majority of black women married to white men that I have interviewed have been in egalitarian marriages which undoubtedly contributed to marital stability and longevity.

DENISE AND TODD

Denise and Todd met through his black ex-girlfriend, who happened to be Denise's best friend. Denise was recently divorced from her first husband, who also was white and by whom she had a son.

Denise's girlfriend had dated Todd several years earlier and thought that Denise and he had a lot in common. At the time, Denise was still married to her first husband and in graduate school. At a party her friend held following Denise's divorce, she introduced her to Todd. According to Denise, the attraction was instant and they spent the entire party together. When the party ended, Denise and Todd made plans to get together a few days later. The next day when

Denise called her friend to thank her for introducing her to Todd, she learned that Todd had already called to thank her for introducing him to Denise. Her friend told her, "Todd was the guy I kept trying to introduce you to two years ago."

Before Todd, the only other white man Denise had dated had been her former husband. Todd, on the other hand, had previously dated several women of color. He preferred darker skinned women. Todd is tall, blond and very 'North Shore' in appearance.

I asked Denise what Todd thought about her already having a child. Denise responded that this was never an issue for him, but it was for his family.

Denise and Todd had a whirlwind courtship. They met in September; for her October birthday, his gift was a trip with him anywhere in the world. She chose Costa Rica because she knew he liked fishing and she enjoyed sitting on the beach. While in Costa Rica, Todd proposed and they married the following May at his parent's North Shore suburban home.

I asked Denise if Todd's family accepted her. She responded that his parents had to deal with her not only being African American but also, they assumed she was from a lower socioeconomic background. Denise recounted an incident that occurred during her wedding reception with one of Todd's longtime white girlfriends. This woman approached Denise at the reception and said, "Denise, you know, I am so proud of Todd for marrying you" and went on along this vein. Denise said the implication was that somehow Todd had 'saved' her, and had married someone he could 'lift up.'

Denise added that while she was shocked at what the woman said, "You never know how racism will come out in your friends until it does." She told Todd about the exchange with this woman and he was first surprised and then angry. Todd had known this woman for most of his life and had never detected any racist feelings. However, as Denise said, "I didn't know how prejudiced some of my black friends were either until they learned I was marrying a white man."

Denise further described her relationship with Todd's parents. She qualified her remarks at the outset by noting, "Most parents would have trouble accepting the news that their child was marrying someone of another race who had been married before and who had a child, and who they had only known for a few months. In fact, without the racial aspect, I would be concerned about that…I would wonder, are you crazy?"

When she first met Todd, he lived in a nice home in Wrigleyville. (A neighborhood on Chicago's north side) She lived on Chicago's southwest side and was working on some community projects. Working on the southwest side gave her a greater appreciation for economic disparities. She wondered how Todd could afford to live in a nice home in a good neighborhood when he was in graduate school and only teaching part-time.

One night when they had been dating for about a month, Todd brought up the subject of meeting his family. The way he approached this conversation made her wary. He started by saying, "Let me tell you about my family," and she thought *uh-oh*. He went on to explain that he grew up in Winnetka and his family had more than most other people. Denise observed that not being from the North Shore, she didn't have any frame of reference for what this meant. Further, this initial meeting would occur during a time when she was wearing her hair in dreadlocks so she knew she would stand out in this way, too.

Todd drove Denise to what she now calls 'the compound'—a large, beautiful home backed up against the golf course with a winding circular driveway. Todd's parents and a few of their friends came out the front door to greet them. She said they were all overly friendly in that phony way, and asked her several questions about herself and her family. "Where do you come from, what do they (her parents) do…questions anyone would ask, but you could tell that they were digging trying to find out as much as possible. What stands out to me from our first meeting was how incredibly phony all of them were. It was really difficult for them."

By contrast, Denise recalled that when she met her first husband's family, they made no effort to pretend they had to like her. She said, "They were redneck country folks, and you can take us or leave us." But Todd's family had a hard time because "it's against their upper middle class sensibilities to be racist. So the bigoted things they have said without thinking they were…and when I would tell them in a nice way that this was racist, they would respond…oh no. And the worst part was that I was an affront to them because I could feel them thinking, *Oh, she's really smart, we had better watch our mouths.*"

It took Todd's family several years to realize that she was not intimidated by them. During that time period, she got rid of her dreadlocks, which her in-laws persisted in calling 'braids.' In the early years of her marriage, every time Todd and she would go home after visiting his family, she was exhausted. However, life issues over the course of their marriage have resolved a lot of the family issues, and she taught them how to treat her. She noted that with her first husband's family, she didn't worry about any of this and attributes the difference 'purely to social class.'

When her in-laws met her son from her first marriage, "They exclaimed how lucky she was that he was so handsome, and that he looked Latino or Asian Indian. No idea how this sounded...like if he looked African American, he wouldn't be handsome." Denise said her in-laws would say the 'dumbest shit' to their two children when they were small, which she had to watch out for. "The implication was that the whiter or more non-black they looked, the better they were."

I asked Denise what her family thought about Todd. Denise responded that her mother was upset when she told her she was getting married again. She thought it was too soon, she didn't know Todd well enough to do this, and that she should finish school and concentrate on raising her son. Further, her mother hoped that she would find a black man to marry. Denise's father, on the other hand, liked Todd, especially because Todd was a golfer like him. Denise pointed out, though, that when Todd met her father, he was in the beginning stages of Alzheimer's, so he wasn't that aware of what was going on. Denise's brother is married to a white woman her mother likes, so race was not a key concern for them.

Denise added that initially her mother had a problem with Todd's mother. Her mother is a very private person and Todd's mother is very inquisitive. As Denise said, "[ ] has way too much time on her hands." Todd's mother had never worked outside of the home and her mother did. "My family instilled a strong work ethic in me and so, of course, did Todd's, but the reality was that he knew he didn't have to work as hard as other people. He was going to inherit a lot of money."

Over the years, Denise has developed a 'wonderful relationship' with her in-laws. As Denise stated, "When it really mattered, Todd's family was right there for us." When her father died, Todd's mother called her mother every day for a week and then several times a week the following month. She made time to visit her mother and take her out. They could not have been more supportive, and her mother appreciated their efforts. When Denise's oldest son got into some trouble, her in-laws stepped in right away to help. Without any judgment or asking questions, her in-laws volunteered to pay for an expensive program to help her son. They told Denise that "[ ] is family; we help each other. That's what money is for."

Those two events were turning points in Denise's relationship with her in-laws. Denise stated…"As life happens, people change… and that includes me changing toward them, too. It took a long time for all of us to reach this point, but it was worth it." As of this writing, Denise and Todd have been married for nearly 20 years.

CHANTELLE AND GLEN

Chantelle is a thirty-five-year-old recording artist who has been married for seven years to Glen, who is thirty-seven and completing his PhD in earth sciences. Chantelle dated Glen for about seven years before they got married. Chantelle is from New Orleans and Glen is from Los Angeles.

Chantelle described growing up in New Orleans, one of six children. She didn't have many interactions with whites and primarily stayed in her own black neighborhood. When she was 19 years old, she got her first recording contract and had to move to Los Angeles. She eventually moved to a small suburb of Los Angeles near the ocean, where she enjoyed the laid-back, peaceful vibe in the neighborhood. "It was the kind of place where you could go to the grocery store in your swimsuit and flip flops and feel perfectly comfortable."

Chantelle admits to being a 'free spirit' and likes 'looking different.' She enjoyed the attention she attracted when she would "go to the beach and be the darkest, most exotic woman there." Rather than try to blend into the crowd, she would always wear white swimsuits which "showed off the contrast between me and the rest of the women there." Chantelle recalled not always feeling good about herself, suffering from low self-esteem when she was younger. However, she decided by the time she moved to California, that "I'm going to embrace it [her skin color] and play it up, you know."

It was while she was walking her miniature poodle in a white dress that showed off how fit she was that she first caught a glimpse of Glen. She had passed by the local fitness center when she saw Glen pull out of the parking lot. He drove by her very slowly, giving her ample time to get a good look at him. For a moment their eyes locked. Chantelle thought he was one of the most handsome men she had ever seen and suspected that he was an actor. She continued walking down the street when suddenly she saw him do a U-turn, driving back down the block to where she was still walking. He pulled over to the curb and stopped his car. He then said to her, "I just have to ask, who are you and where are you from?" Chantelle said he looked at her as if she was from the planet Mars. "And we stopped right there in that one spot for like an hour and a half, like time stood still, as if we had known each other forever." Chantelle laughingly remembers her little poodle getting very tired and just lying down on the sidewalk. By this time, she had learned Glen's name, and "he [Glen] sees that my dog is on her back so he just starts rubbing her belly. I was so enraptured. And even to this day, we go back to that little sidewalk point sometimes and remember."

I asked Chantelle if this was the first white male to whom she had been attracted. Chantelle responded by describing a conversation she and an older woman friend had about men when she was in her late teens. The friend told her, "Chantelle, know your market, know your market. And I was like, what does that mean?" Her friend responded that she would figure it out eventually. Chantelle thought her 'market' was her New Orleans neighborhood until she realized by her first year of college that "these guys [black males]—I'm not ideal to them. To them, I am not attractive, or at least not attractive enough for them to want to date me."

One of Chantelle's first singing tours was to England, where she started to wonder what was wrong with her, why no one liked her. In her mind, 'no one' was the black men from her neighborhood. She started praying, asking God to send her a sign that she was beautiful. A few evenings later, she was in a London cab which was stopped by the light. While waiting for the light to change, an older, very well-dressed white man walked across the street in front of the cab and looked directly at her. He stopped walking, looked her in the eye, smiled softly, and then continued walking. After he crossed the street, he looked back at her again and smiled once more. According to Chantelle, "in that moment, I said he's beautiful because he thought I was beautiful. So the transfer just happened. That was the awakening for me. I said to myself, 'Oh, this is my market'. This is my market." This experience changed Chantelle. When she returned to the United States, she no longer focused on black men. "If a black male didn't roll over and fall out over me, I didn't even notice because I had discovered that there were other men in the world who found me to be beautiful."

I asked Chantelle what other experiences she had with black men. She recounted being teased as a child by a boy who called her 'Celie.' Celie was the character in the movie *The Color Purple* who was unattractive and had experienced several degrading incidences and sexual abuse from black men. "And to a girl who's still trying to discover herself, Celie is the furthest from, you know, desirable. And so, you know, it takes a long time to get over something like that once the seed's been planted in your head. So I struggled with that, like maybe I look like, you know, this Celie to these guys...and that was a negative."

Chantelle recalled also that one time she did date a black man who was a record producer. She noticed that he liked her to wear her hair long and straight, and he treated her better when she did. He was not as complimentary when she wore her hair natural or in a short Afro. She felt he was embarrassed by her appearance when she didn't have her hair weaved. He would want to stay at home and order carry-out. She thought it was disrespectful and simple-minded to base one's interest in a woman on how she wore her hair. The relationship didn't last very long because she felt this man had his mind set on a certain type of black woman, a certain look, that she didn't have.

By contrast, Glen told her that he found the 'little curls on her neck' beautiful. Chantelle described what happened when she became ill a few months into their relationship and could not pull herself together to look decent. Glen came over while her hair was in cornrows ("and not neat ones either because I had not been up to doing my hair") and she reluctantly opened the front door. He proceeded to help her and told her she didn't look as bad as she felt. When Chantelle told her mother that Glen had seen 'her nappy kitchen', her mother burst out laughing and said, "If that man loves your nappy kitchen, you be sure and hold on to him."

I asked Chantelle how her siblings and father felt about her relationship with Glen. She recounted putting Glen to the test with one of her brothers. She forewarned Glen that this brother would try to break him down and see what he was made of and if he didn't like Glen, it would be a problem. Chantelle took Glen to meet her brother at a local New Orleans bar, "a place that few white people would ever go to." She then left Glen to run an errand. When she returned about forty-five minutes later, she heard her brother telling Glen that if he needed anything (while in New Orleans) to let him know. She was somewhat surprised, thinking her brother might eventually come around to accepting Glen, but not that soon. It turned out that for whatever reason 'the two of them clicked' and they have been on good terms ever since.

As for her father, Chantelle said that as long as she was happy, he was happy. Of her siblings, her second brother and two of her sisters have dated people outside their race. However, her youngest sister doesn't feel comfortable dating outside her race. Chantelle attributes this to the fact that her sister hasn't ever left the neighborhood. "She keeps trying to make her relationship with her current boyfriend work...and it does for a while, and then it is off again."

Chantelle stated that when she gets negative looks they are usually from either a white woman or a black man. According to Chantelle, "white women look at me and I know they must wonder how Glen wound up with me [because he is very good looking] and black men give me angry looks, like, why are you with that white dude."

Chantelle and her husband are looking forward to having children. She stated that for the time being her career comes first. She doesn't have the time to take off yet, even though she knows her peak childbearing years are limited. However, her husband and she tease, "We want to have either a little Halle Berry or a little Obama, or maybe even both, you know."

Postscript on Chantelle: Glen and she adopted a child a year ago and recently Chantelle gave birth to their second child.

ALYCE AND ANDREW

Alyce and Andrew are from the Milwaukee area and met at the University of Minnesota through their respective roommates, who were a couple. Now in their mid-thirties, married for nearly ten years and with two young children, they are both working professionals. Alyce is an attorney and Andrew is an information technology specialist.

Alyce and Andrew started our interview by discussing life in Minnesota, where interracial couples are fairly common around the Minneapolis area. Alyce has older relatives who are interracially married so it was not a big deal for her to date a white man. She also has two female cousins her age who date interracially. When I asked Alyce if she had any negative experiences while dating Andrew, she responded, "Yes, I did...mostly looks from black people on the street" in the Milwaukee area. In Minnesota, she recalled going with Andrew to a movie theater, "and there was this black guy sitting there, and we were going to sit by him, and he lifted the seats. He didn't want to sit by us."

I asked Alyce and Andrew if they had experienced any negative or positive social interactions from white people when they were out together. Alyce responded that "with white people, it was different. The reaction would be more...there was always an assumption we weren't together. I think it didn't occur to them that we were a couple."

Andrew agreed with his wife's perception and provided another example. One time they had gone to the Drake hotel (in downtown Chicago) for her father's birthday party. He was holding their son and the baby stroller while Alyce spoke to one of the concierges. Another concierge approached and asked if he needed any help, despite the fact that he was standing next to Alyce. Apparently the second concierge didn't think they were together. Andrew noted that both concierges were older white men and perhaps 'it just didn't click with them that Alyce and I would be a couple.'

Neither Andrew nor Alyce felt they had experienced hostile reactions to their relationship, but noted that people at times were surprised when they found out they were in an interracial marriage. Andrew stated that when his black co-workers discovered he had a black wife, he felt they warmed up to him more quickly. He thought their social exchanges were more open and honest. As for his white co-workers, he didn't think any of them cared who he was married to.

The one problem Alyce runs into is that at times she has been mistaken for her children's nanny by whites. However, she recalled being in a shopping center parking lot with her infant daughter when another black woman parked in the same area began to call out to her. When the woman approached, she said, "I just want to know, do you work for a service or do you work directly for the family? I'm looking for a job, too. And I was like, she's my daughter. And the woman was really embarrassed and apologized. But this was the first time a black person had thought that, too."

Alyce went on to say that when Andrew and she discussed having children, it was important to her that he realize their children would be considered black. Andrew didn't have any problem with this; however, both of their children appear to be white. As Andrew pointed out, "[ ] looks just like me when I was his age, but with a tan." Their toddler daughter has straight black hair with blue eyes.

The lack of any visible black ancestry in their children was a surprise for Alyce. She maintains that in her mind, "my children are black, or at least mixed...even if they don't appear that way." Alyce is light brown-skinned, but acknowledged that she comes from a fair-skinned family. Andrew laughed at his wife's frustration while stating, "Hey, who wants to argue about genetics…these are our children and this is the way they look; so what? They are healthy and beautiful and that is what matters most."

When I asked Alyce and Andrew how their families felt about their relationship, Andrew responded that basically they came from similar families. Alyce readily agreed by stating that their parents were on the same page politically, they grew up in similar neighborhoods, and other than the fact she was raised as a Lutheran and Andrew as Catholic, not much else stood out as differences between them. When their children were born, Andrew's mother came to help out for a few weeks until they were able to adjust to the new schedule.

Alyce noted Andrew and she still had many of the same friends, but acknowledged that one of her black female friends was not accepting of her relationship. Alyce knew this friend disapproved of their marriage and began to keep her at a distance. Over time the relationship ended, which Alyce does not regret. "If someone doesn't accept your spouse for no reason other than their own racial hang-ups, that's their problem, not mine." Alyce and Andrew ended the interview by noting that they were glad they lived in a community which was welcoming of interracial couples and where they had made many new friends.

SHARON AND JACK

Jack is in his middle 50s and his wife Sharon is in her middle 40s. They are attorneys and this is the second marriage for both of them. They have known each other for many years because they work in the same large government office. Theirs was initially a strictly business relationship; they were in the same position in the office but worked out of different locations. At one time, Sharon's sister had been Jack's boss, but by the time they started dating, Jack no longer worked for her. Sharon has worked in the office for about six years, Jack for about thirteen years.

Jack started the interview by noting that he had been attracted to Sharon for a long time but didn't know how to approach her. He asked one of Sharon's white colleagues and somewhat of a mutual friend, "What's the deal with your friend Sharon?" The colleague responded, "You stay away from her; she doesn't date anyone from work." Sharon stated that she was very strict about following work rules and not dating anyone with whom she had to work. She had worked hard to get where she was professionally, and she didn't want to do anything to undermine her career progress. As Sharon said, "I am all about the work persona, being professional."

It was about a year later when they were assigned to the same team at work that they started talking to each other. Sharon learned that Jack and she had gone through their divorces at around the same time and his youngest child was the same age as her older son, so they began to swap stories.

Sharon recalled her friend telling her about Jack's interest which she was surprised to learn because Jack comes off as "serious, intense, cocky, and arrogant...the chief and his Indians." Once they started exchanging information about their children, her view softened towards him. They had another co-worker who started praising Jack to Sharon, but she still held back because she followed her rule—you don't date coworkers. Eventually, after talking with him so much at work, she said to herself, "Why not consider what's in your face? We are often faced with not knowing who people really are, and I do know a lot about Jack already, so why not give it (dating him) a chance?"

Their first date was at a downtown Chicago restaurant. They had a good time and the relationship developed from there. At the time, Sharon lived about 50 miles from Jack and she was impressed that he never complained about driving her home after they went out.

Their former spouses were from their same ethnic groups: Sharon's husband was African American; Jack's wife was Jewish. I asked them if there was anything different they were doing in this marriage and if race played any role. Jack responded by noting, "Yes, I thought about race, and what people would say in the beginning, but by the time the relationship became serious, maybe I was naïve, or just didn't care enough anymore; Sharon is intelligent, hardworking, beautiful—how could I go wrong with that?" Laughing, Sharon readily agreed with him.

Jack further noted that growing up, his mother wanted him to marry a Jewish girl, and he did, but as he got older, his mother's wishes didn't matter as much to him.

Sharon said that Jack's race was not an issue for her. Most important to her was whether or not Jack was a good person and that they were on the same page. She noted, "I am a private person, all about my work persona. Even if he had been African American, I would have the same concerns. Jack is into his children, my children, and he keeps up with what is important to them. That made a great impression on me. He is a good person. Being a single mother, that was most important to me." Moreover, no one from her family objected to her marrying Jack.

Jack said his children initially objected to his marriage "not because Sharon is black but because they wondered what my priorities would be with a new wife. Nothing race related with my children." Both of his parents liked Sharon, his late father in particular. He kept encouraging Sharon to promote herself more at work because he thought she was so smart. Jack described his mother as a 'harder nut to crack' and being a Holocaust survivor definitely affected her personality.

Sharon observed that from the time she met Jack's parents, they treated her warmly and with open arms. When Jack and she visited them in Florida in the winter and went to a country club where she was the only 'chocolate drop' there, she felt perfectly fine and included.

I asked Sharon and Jack if their former spouses were involved in their children's lives. Sharon responded that her ex-husband is not involved in their child's life currently due to issues between her son and his father, nothing to do with her spouse. She is glad her son has Jack in his life.

Sharon and Jack described some advantages and positive social reactions to their interracial marriage. Sharon observed that she has a good friend who considers her a big sister and who hasn't had any dating success. "Now that she sees me married to Jack, this has broadened her mindset as to who she thinks she can date." Sharon stated that in their marriage, Jack and she use their ethnicities to their advantage. For example, a situation may arise at work she thinks a white person should handle; other times a black person may manage a situation better.

Jack believes one positive reaction to their relationship is that in their 2000-person office, once they started dating (and the office is run primarily by African American women), he noticed he was perceived differently. Their relationship "perhaps humanized" him to others, and he was promoted. He attributes this in large part to watching how Sharon handles people, which made him more self-confident in how he approached others.

When I inquired about negative reactions to their relationship, Jack replied that he was the one to hear racist comments. They live just east of a section in Chicago which is still primarily white and racist. One time when they went to a restaurant in this area, Jack overheard another restaurant patron utter 'nigger lover' under his breath when Sharon and he were being seated. He ignored the comment because he didn't want to start anything in a restaurant. The same thing happened when they were parked at a convenience store in the area.

Most of the time Jack and Sharon leave the neighborhood to go downtown to socialize, where they haven't run into any negative situations. As an experiment, Jack once took Sharon to an event where he knew she would probably be the only black person and she took him to an event where he would be the only white person. Sharon said that Jack commented on being uncomfortable as the only white person and she told him, "Welcome to my world. Black people are in this situation far more often than the reverse." Jack wrote a blog about his experience.

Sharon observed that sometimes black people think when she is with Jack that he is '5-0', meaning the police. "He has that look with the way he dresses and the cap he wears." He once walked into a beauty salon where she was having her hair done and the other women thought he was a police officer. This perception caused some tension among the other customers until they started to figure out that Jack and she were together. Other than that, Sharon hasn't had any negative social experiences with Jack. As she stated, "I am comfortable with who I am so I really don't think about it (what other people may think)."

When I asked Jack and Sharon if there was anything else they thought it was important for me to know about their interracial marriage, Jack responded, "There is marriage, and there are second marriages with children involved." This is the biggest concern the two of them have. Jack and Sharon have a five-year-old daughter and he noted that the way his older children from his first marriage were raised was different. Sharon readily agreed with Jack's remark and said that the same thing goes for how she raised her older children as well.

Jack stated that the way he was with his older children colors his experience and he is learning to adjust to not only having another child, but also the cultural differences between his two wives. "You have to be able to adjust to how your spouse has raised their children." Marriages may be easier when there are no children. Parenting is probably the biggest cultural difference between them.

Jack and Sharon discussed how they grew up and how they raised their children. Juggling all of their older children, ranging in age from 20 to 31, is important and requires a lot of effort. "You have to be present for what they are going through all of the time." Sharon agreed and told a story about how her older son is dating a white girl from Martinsville, Indiana (the birthplace of the Ku Klux Klan). "It is interesting to see the evolution of their relationship against the backdrop of historical racism. We both talk to him about it." Jack ended the interview by stating that learning how Sharon and her family express themselves has been a positive experience and made him a better person.

CYNTHIA AND TOM

Cynthia and Tom are both in their early 50s and have been married for ten years. Cynthia is from the South and Tom grew up on Chicago's North Shore. Cynthia is a social worker and Tom works in human resources at a local company. This is their first marriage.

They met at a Friday night fellowship group. As a single woman, Cynthia attended this group night frequently with friends and noticed that Tom accompanied an older man who was wheelchair bound. She observed how patient he was with him and this sparked an immediate attraction to Tom. As Cynthia noted, "In my dating history, the characteristics that I chose for a male were basically based on aesthetics and this time, because I am older, I wanted someone who would be there for me when the 'pretty' was gone. And I saw Tom demonstrate that when he was patient with this man. He would wheel him. He never got angry. We would go out to dinner. He would help feed him or, you know, dab his mouth with a napkin if needed; he was very attentive and patient. I was very attracted to him. So that's how we met, and we dated for about two years before we got married."

Cynthia was the one who made the initial move in the relationship. She asked Tom if he would like to go out sometime after one of the fellowship meetings. Tom described Cynthia as being very nervous when she asked if he would like to get coffee and donuts. He was also surprised, because "I had come to the conclusion I wasn't meant to get married or have that kind of long-term relationship. I had had one long-term one that I knew wasn't going to pan out." When they got married, in honor of their first date at a Dunkin Donuts, and the place where Tom proposed to her, they decided to use the donut shop colors as a part of their wedding color scheme.

I asked the couple if racial issues impacted their relationship. Cynthia responded, "I have to say, I never even thought about it. Of course, I know Tom is Caucasian. I mean, I'm looking at him, and I see him, but I never even thought about it, so much so that when I started dating him, and I would tell my best friend about him, I never even mentioned his race. And I don't know if she [her best friend] assumed he was black. I don't know what she thought because we never talked about it. Tom is not an African American name, although some men are Thomas. But it just never came up. So when she found out he was white, she said, "That's curious, you never mentioned it." And it didn't affect our relationship at all. It was just a non-factor, you know. I wasn't like, 'Ooh girl, he's white. What do you think?' It was just normal for me."

Tom said he was never concerned that Cynthia was black; she was not the first black woman he had dated. In fact, he had dated Puerto Ricans, Hispanics, and Asians, too. He stated that he was aware, though, there were people who might give him a problem, so he was careful about places where he thought he could run into trouble. "But as far as Cynthia and me getting together, it [race] was never a consideration. Yeah, in fact, I think it's just the opposite. I think it enhances our relationship. It makes it richer."

Cynthia noted that Tom and she "have had very spirited conversations about race and how it impacts us, how I look through things with a different lens. Like sometimes Tom and I will take a road trip, and he'll turn into a driveway. And I have a different visceral response to that than he does. He just thinks, oh, I'm making a three-point turn. It's no big deal. I'm like, we're in somebody's private driveway. They'll look in, they'll see me; we, you know, I get nervous, I get tense. I get concerned. And he has a different experience, so we talk about it. He doesn't dismiss or diminish my concern. But I let him know, it's just a very different experience for me, those kinds of situations, even though I was born and raised in Evanston. My parents are from the South, and I kind of live vicariously through some of their experiences that they've shared with me about being in certain neighborhoods and being black. So I still have those thoughts. There's a residual. I'm always looking through a lens with that in mind."

Cynthia and Tom both said that no one in either of their families objected to their relationship. In fact, Cynthia's older brother performed their marriage ceremony. Her father is deceased and her mother lives in the South and has told several of her friends that

"Cynthia married a white man…and you know that's big news where she lives." Cynthia and Tom share their home with her unmarried sister, and according to the couple, all three of them get along fine. Tom's mother is deceased and his father remarried. He does not have a close relationship with his father. While his brother likes Cynthia, his sister has been distant from Tom for many years and especially since his marriage. Tom shrugged his shoulders and said of his sister, "If this is the way she wants to be, so be it. Not my problem."

Cynthia and Tom observed that their friends are very accepting of their relationship. As Cynthia noted, "I have few friends to begin with and if any of them didn't respect my relationship that would end the friendship." The couple go out with several of Tom's friends.

Due to the nature of Cynthia's work, she felt compelled to tell her African American women clients that she was marrying a white man. "They were single women and looking for relationships and I didn't want the fact I was marrying a white man to diminish or tarnish or weaken our professional relationship. I didn't want them to think I was less of a black woman because I was marrying someone that is not black. So I brought this up in that context." Cynthia indicated that her clients accepted her news and thanked her for telling them. All of those clients are still working with her.

I asked Cynthia and Tom to further elaborate on what attracted them to each other. Cynthia responded that seeing how gentle and patient Tom was served as an opportunity for her to explore how mature she had become; she was looking for character traits that had longevity. She wanted someone who was emotionally stable.

According to Cynthia, "That's what I saw in Tom, a consistency. That's what I was attracted to."

For Tom, Cynthia was "really cute when we started dating, and she's only gotten cuter. She's a beautiful woman externally, but she's also very beautiful on the inside as well. And to be perfectly honest with you, I think her internal beauty to me was a bigger attraction. And I don't just say that because it sounds nice. You know, it is the truth. She's a person of integrity. I'm sort of the opposite. I tend to take shortcuts, okay?" Tom laughed and continued by saying that he has integrity, just a different version from Cynthia. Tom concluded his thoughts on why he was attracted to Cynthia by saying, "Cynthia is a by-the-book kind of person. And I admire that, I truly do. And also her intellect. She's clearly highly intelligent and we have great conversations, but not just about race, other issues, too. So I feel like I got the whole package."

Cynthia and Tom think that being older when they met helped their relationship. As Cynthia stated, "By the time you reach your forties, you have had time to get to know yourself and are just interested in creating your own personal happiness. You aren't as distracted by what other people may think or say."

Tom agreed with Cynthia and noted that when he was growing up his parents lived in an affluent community only because his grandparents helped out financially. He remembers "feeling like eyes were on me all of the time, you know, judgmental eyes." As a result of feeling like the outsider, he has a greater sensitivity to racial nuances.

I asked Cynthia and Tom if there was anything else that they thought important to address about their interracial marriage. Tom said he had heard of the stereotype that a white man would only marry a black woman because something was wrong with him; perhaps he was impotent, so he settled for a black woman. Tom laughed when he stated that "nothing could be further from the truth" in his relationship with Cynthia.

Cynthia responded to this question by noting she has heard the stereotype that black women marry white men for money. "That's the only reason they can be together. That's the only thing she could find remotely interesting about him. He must have some money. Her response to that if she were ever asked would be 'Well, doesn't everybody have some money?' I mean, a dollar is some money, you know? Tom and I measure wealth other than by a decimal point in our financial portfolio. There's such a thing as spiritual currency and spiritual wealth. To me, those are equally important."

KAREN AND JESSE

Karen and Jesse are in their middle 30s and have been married for ten years. Both of them recently completed their PhDs in science fields. Karen works part-time so she can care for their two young children. Jesse works full-time in a lab. They both grew up in Michigan; Karen in suburban Detroit and Jesse in a small northern rural town. Karen and Jesse met in college. Karen's white roommate, who had known Jesse prior to college, thought that the two of them should meet each other because they had a lot in common. One day when Jesse stopped by their dorm room, Karen answered the door and they started talking. They continued to get together for various campus events and subsequently started dating. Karen was the first African American woman Jesse had dated; Karen had dated men from a variety of ethnic groups. She also mentioned that when she was younger she identified as bisexual.

Karen noted the dorm where she lived on campus was very progressive and that her dating Jesse was not any big deal.

Jesse and Karen attended different universities for graduate school but their relationship continued. As their relationship became more serious, they met each other's families. When Karen took Jesse home to meet her parents, her mother was very standoffish. She didn't warm-up to Jesse at first. Moreover, the night she went home was her parents' official 'date night' and her father didn't want to cancel their plans. Her mother, however, convinced him to wait for Karen and Jesse to arrive. Her dad was just barely polite to Jesse, and her mother noticed how upset Karen was with her father's behavior. Later that evening, her mother softened her tone, telling Karen, "I can see that you really love this boy." Her mother began to treat Jesse well, while Karen's father was unmoved. He lectured Karen about the treatment of black people in general, and black women in particular, at the hands of white men.

Karen stated, "My dad took another two years to warm up to Jesse, not only because Jesse is white, but I think also, he didn't think most men would be good enough for his daughter." The other part was that he thought Jesse was out for what he called a 'black experience.' "He thought Jesse just wanted to say he dated a black girl, but then once my dad realized that this was not the case, he was just sort of like, well, he's a guy. Over time he realized that he actually liked Jesse."

Jesse's parents were no more welcoming of Karen. When he told his mother that Karen was African American, she reminded him that his stepfather would not be very happy about this. However, she said to Jesse, "What does it really matter?" Jesse's stepsister was involved in a serious relationship with a black man and her father disowned her. He told Jesse that he wasn't racist, but he just didn't think blacks and whites should date or intermarry.

When Jesse told his own father that Karen was African American, he immediately began to lecture him about how hard his life would be if he married a black woman. Jesse took Karen to meet his mother on an evening when he didn't think his stepfather would be home. Unfortunately, his stepfather came home early and the four of them endured a very awkward and uncomfortable dinner. Karen remembers that Jesse's stepfather would not look at her. Jesse's mother made a sincere effort to get to know Karen over the next year; however, Karen said that being around Jesse's stepfather was too uncomfortable for her so she didn't go back to their home. Later Karen learned that Jesse's stepfather had said some very derogatory things about her.

Jesse's younger sister also dates African American men or other men of color. Jesse said that this caused a lot of tension in his mother's marriage—all three of the children were dating African Americans. This tension undoubtedly was one of the contributing factors to his mother's divorce from his stepfather. Jesse's father, while disapproving of their relationship, eventually 'got used to it.'

Karen had aunts and uncles who made it clear that they didn't like her dating a white man. Much like her father, one of her uncles told her, "How can you date a white man after all of the horrible things they have done to us?" Karen said, "And you know, my parents—at first my dad didn't want to say anything; he won't challenge his relatives, but my mom was like, 'that has nothing to do with Jesse.' About a year later, my dad started basically agreeing with my mom that Jesse shouldn't be blamed for the past."

Jesse and Karen have a number of friends that are in interracial relationships. The only group to which Karen belonged that had any problems with her relationship with Jesse was a support group for LGBTQ (Lesbian, Gay, Bisexual, Transgender, and Questioning) students of color. Karen was surprised and annoyed at the number of gay black men who had concerns about her dating a white man. She hadn't received any negative feedback from straight black men. She took Jesse to one of the group meetings and not surprisingly, once several of the members met and talked with him, they changed their minds.

In the years since their marriage, Jesse stated that Karen's family treats him like family. He thinks "they have basically just forgotten that I am white. They don't alter their conversations around me at all." At times the racial conversations can become quite heated and then one of the relatives might look over at him and say, "Jesse, you know we don't mean you at all."

Some of Jesse's family is still fairly awkward around Karen, and at times say things that they don't mean to sound the way they do. For example, at one of the family picnics, one of Jesse's cousins remarked plaintively to Karen about "how dark her children were getting being out in the sun." Jesse has an elderly uncle who in his efforts to make

Karen feel welcome made some sexist remarks about women, and then told Karen to let him know if Jesse ever started cheating on her.

Jesse stated that he would never live back in rural northern Michigan because the people there are never going to be accepting of interracial couples. In Chicago, Karen and he have felt disapproving stares from older black women and white men. Karen added that "younger people basically do not care."

I asked Karen and Jesse what advice they would give to other couples considering dating and marrying interracially. They responded that the key to their relationship is that they talked about racial issues right from the beginning. "You have to have open and honest communication, otherwise there will be too much stress in the relationship." They also mentioned that there were several places they would not travel to, mostly small rural towns, as an interracial couple. They aren't willing to expose their children and themselves to possible racial trouble. When they drove to Mississippi to visit some of Karen's family, they made reservations beforehand at hotels along the route so there wouldn't be any surprises. As Jesse noted, "in small towns you may find more overt racists than in larger cities."

Jesse added that at work he has a photo of his wife and family on his desk so his co-workers know Karen is African American. Karen met some of them one time when she stopped by his office. Only one coworker has ever commented on his family and nothing else has been said to him.

The only racial issue Karen and Jesse are concerned about in their marriage is making certain their children get exposed to and are comfortable in both cultures. Other than this, they noted how much the two of them have in common, which they believe makes their relationship successful. As Karen pointed out, "I am a scientist, I am interested in the same kind of research Jesse is, we have the same education level, and we share similar interests and hobbies—at the end of the day, race shouldn't keep you apart." Jesse added, "I have far more in common with Karen than I would with a white woman from my rural hometown with a tenth grade education. We have each other's back so we make it work."

DEANNE AND DARREN

Deanne is fifty years old and her husband Darren is forty-three. They have been married for eight years, after dating for five years. Deanne works as a personal trainer while Darren is a mechanical engineer. She is originally from New Jersey and Darren is from the Midwest. They met online.

Deanne began the interview by telling me that she was raised Jewish. Her father was African American and Swiss and she remembers that his parents were practicing Jews, too. She grew up in a predominantly white New Jersey community with few African Americans. As a result, she was more comfortable around whites than blacks as a young person. She recalled growing up hearing several stereotypes about black men which further caused her to distance herself from them.

She didn't date until she went to college, and her first boyfriend was white. She also briefly dated two black men while in college, but felt that "there was just something missing, plus there was still the fact that there were these stereotypes I had in the back of my mind." I asked Deanne what stereotypes she was referring to, and she responded, "Stereotypes that black men always cheated, that a lot of black marriages did not last long."

After she graduated from college, she took a job as an administrator at a construction company. One of the white workers was attracted to her and eventually asked her to go out with him. Deanne enjoyed his company and they became an 'item.' They wound up dating for about five years and according to Deanne they were all but married. I asked her why the relationship ended to which Deanne responded, "I did love him, but there was just one barrier I couldn't get over—I needed the education. My father was an entrepreneur, a head biochemist at Hoffman LaRoche, became self-employed— I just wanted someone with more ambition." Also, she said that her parents liked him, but "they never thought he was good enough for me."

Deanne didn't date for two years after her first relationship ended. However, she met a chef who was African American and after dating him for two years, they got married. She readily admits that she was not ready to get married when she did. "I got married because all of my girlfriends were getting married and I started thinking that if I wanted kids, plus a job I am happy with, and finding my place in life…all of this is going to take time. So I know I married for the wrong reasons. My parents told me I wasn't ready, but you think you know everything when you are young. The marriage lasted three years."

One factor which hastened the end of her marriage was that Deanne became pregnant. She had been diagnosed with diabetes, thus her doctor was concerned that the pregnancy could kill her or the baby. At one of Deanne's doctor visits, fortunately when her mother was with her, he told them his concerns about her continuing with the pregnancy. He suggested that Deanne have an abortion to ensure her health and her mother readily agreed with him. Deanne said that between having an abortion and not being happy living where she was, the marriage broke up shortly thereafter.

Following her divorce, Deanne said that she took a hiatus from dating for nearly eight years. During this time she worked on her career and spent a lot of time with her many gay friends. Deanne remarked that she had a busy life in New York City between her work, her two dogs and going out with friends. She indicated that she was not the kind of person who just had to have a man in her life.

One day Darren contacted her on Match.com. Deanne had never removed her profile from this online dating site. Darren had contacted her before but she had ignored him for about three months. She was like "uh, another man, you know, I don't need that right now. I'm happy where I am. I just want to live my life now." Darren then sent her another email which said, "Well, I guess you are not interested. I'll leave you alone." So then, she started to think that maybe she should meet him in person; "if nothing else, it would be a free dinner." They met at a restaurant near her home and had a ball.

Deanne described walking into the restaurant where Darren was already seated at a table. I asked about her initial impression of him. Deanne described Darren as being so much more attractive than his Internet photo. "On Match.com, he looked like a nerd, a total homely nerd. In person, he was very physically attractive. I was shocked…and then I thought, *How can a man this attractive be attracted to me?*" I asked Deanne why she thought that, to which she responded, "Blonde, blue eyes, German." I mentioned to Deanne that several of the black women I had interviewed for this book had specifically noted German men tended to like black women. Deanne replied, "Yeah, so I am learning. Just not what I am used to."

To Deanne's surprise, she learned Darren was a mechanical engineer with a Master's degree in the field. He had grown up in Sheboygan, Wisconsin and received his education from the University of Wisconsin-Platteville. He was hired right out of school by a company that sent him to different locations around the country. They met up while his project assignment was in New Jersey. His career put him in contact with all kinds of people and his boss was impressed with how well he communicated with them. "Darren had the personality that allowed him to work well with everyone."

After their four-hour date ended, Darren asked Deanne if she wanted to go out again. She told him "yes, but I didn't think he was going to follow up so soon, but he called me the next day and the day after that, too." Soon enough they started dating exclusively, which went on for about five years.

Deanne said that while dating Darren, she knew he could be transferred away from New Jersey at any time and one day it happened. Darren told her that he was being transferred back to company headquarters in Chicago. She recalled being sad, but had resolved to put a brave face on for him. She told him, "Well, we both knew this day was coming." He responded, "Well, you know, we don't have to end it here. I'd like for you to come with me." Deanne recalled laughingly that her sugar dropped so low she passed out. As she explained, "Darren's not the type of person to let you know ahead of time what he has on his mind."

Deanne added that after Darren 'brought her back to life' he jokingly told her she had not answered him. "And I'm like what? So he goes, 'well, this is the plan. I want you to stay at my house'—he had a dog. 'I want you to stay at my house because I'm going to be living in Chicago to, you know, become acclimated' and blah, blah, blah. So I'm like, okay."

I asked Deanne what her parents thought about Darren. She replied that her father loved him. "In fact, he said that finally I had met a man worthy of me. So now I have to tell you about my mother. She feels that black women should stay with black men. She's not into interracial marriage. However, when she met Darren, the whole conversation changed."

Deanne moved to Chicago with Darren and decided to pursue work as a personal trainer. She was hired by a company which had excellent benefits and provided great health insurance. However, she had to work 30 hours a week and that became too much for her. "I was working back-to-back. So Darren's like, you're never home. I'm home more than you are. I'm supposed to be the bread winner you know."

Darren encouraged her to apply to an athletic club as a personal trainer. Initially she hesitated to do so because she didn't think this club would be interested in hiring a black woman. The company she worked for was more urban-oriented, while the athletic club was very suburban. To her surprise, she was hired by the athletic club and the best part was that it was close to her home so she spent far less time commuting to work. She quit her first job and had to go on COBRA for health insurance. This is when Darren said to her, "You know, your COBRA is going to run out so we need to get married. So basically we got married so I could be covered under his company's health insurance."

I asked Deanne if marriage had changed their relationship in any way. She replied, "No, I don't think so; at least I can't think of anything. We had been together for so long that nothing really changed."

In terms of Darren's family, Deanne stated that she had met his parents several years earlier. They had traveled to Wisconsin to attend a birthday party for his grandmother. It turned out that his grandmother's birthday was two days before hers, and when the grandmother discovered this fact, she wanted to have a double birthday celebration. Deanne recalled that "Darren's mother and grandmother were welcoming of me right from the start." His father, however, was real quiet around her for the first few days of their visit. By the end of their stay, his father had begun to tease her. He continued to warm up to her and Darren told her that his father was fine with their relationship. Darren's two brothers are married and she gets along well with his sisters-in-law, too. Deanne stated that Darren and she visit his family three to four times a year.

I asked Deanne if there was anything about being in an interracial relationship that she thought other black women should know. Her response: "As far as advice, people are people regardless of what color, shape or size they are. If you have specific criteria—I wanted the education, I wanted a good background—then I would say focus your prejudices on those aspects, not on race or ethnicity. And don't be afraid to say hello to someone outside of your race or your comfort zone. Just do it because people, especially in Illinois and New York, are the friendliest people I've ever met. New Jersey people are snobs."

ANITA AND DON

Anita and Don are in their upper 30s, have been married for nine years and have two children. She is a pharmaceutical representative; Don is an accountant. They met at the health club to which they both belong.

I started the interview by asking them about their backgrounds. Anita described growing up with a strong sense of being African American. Her parents were always involved in social issues which pertained to black life and insisted that her brother and she know their history. When she was a child, her parents took a lot of time instilling a sense of black pride. She recognizes that it was to prepare her to feel confident in a white world. Her mother belonged to the local Jack and Jill chapter, was an active participant in her black sorority as an adult, and had attended a HBCU (historically black college and university). Her father had been fairly politically active during his time at the University of Maryland.

Anita grew up outside of Baltimore in an integrated town and attended public schools, where she did well. When it came time for her to apply to college, her parents encouraged her to enroll at a HBCU. As Anita's mother told her, "Your life will be enriched by an immersion in black culture." While she didn't consciously think about it, she noted that she "liked the idea of being in an all African

American university environment with the possibly of meeting more black men." Taking her mother's advice, she enrolled at an East Coast HBCU.

Don grew up in the same community as Anita but went to a different high school. His parents are divorced but both were active in his life. He said that his parents never got into any long conversations with him about race when he was growing up "and they did have some black friends." Don had two black male friends while in high school and they are still friends today. Don describes his parents as being liberal, having spent years working in government and meeting people from a wide variety of ethnic backgrounds. Don said that he didn't date much in high school because he was very involved in sports. He added that few of his male friends did much dating in high school for the same reason. When he was a senior in high school, he asked one of the girls he shared several classes with if she wanted to go with him to the prom. "It wasn't like we were dating; she wouldn't have considered me a boyfriend, but we both needed someone to go to the prom with, and she was always nice and a cool girl."

Don attended a Big Ten university, where he majored in math. He joined a fraternity but didn't become a 'frat boy.' "Heavy partying and drinking were never my thing. I joined the fraternity to have a group of friends on campus." When he was a junior in college, he got a summer internship at an accounting firm. He made some great connections there, and one of the firm's senior partners became his mentor. Following his college graduation, he was hired in an entry level position and began taking business classes which would allow him to sit for the CPA (Certified Public Accountant) exam.

Don said that he didn't have any serious romantic relationships while in college, but did go out on the weekends with some of his fraternity brothers. "We'd hit a few bars, watch a few games, and call it a night."

I asked Anita if college life met her expectations, to which she replied, "Sort of." She made many new black women friends and joined her mother's sorority, but as far as relationships with black men, "not so much." I asked her to elaborate on this subject to which she responded, "Let's see, first of all, this was the first time that I met so many black men who were gay. Some were openly gay; a few of them were still questioning [their gender identity] or said they were, and one guy, who I am still friends with, is the son of a minister, and he was working on how to tell his father that he was gay. Then there were the nice nerdy-types, straight but not interested in dating or social life that much. Most of these guys were thinking ahead and totally career minded. You might catch them every now and then at a black function or party, but when the party ended, they usually just left…never hung around. I knew two guys who were very political on campus and into black issues, but then I learned one of them had a white girlfriend at another school. And of course, you know, there were some that were just players; they would play women against each other, basically just looking for the booty wherever they could get it."

When she was a senior in college, Anita attended a job fair, where she was recruited by her current employer, a large pharmaceutical company. One of the company's benefits was a reduced membership rate at a nearby health club. She would go to the club on the weekends to unwind and to keep herself in shape. The club had a list of activities that you could sign up for to do as a group. Anita signed up to participate in the running group because she thought this would be a good way to meet new people post-college, and not necessarily connected to her job.

About six months after she joined the health club, she met a black guy who she would see from time to time. He was a few years older than her and invested in his career. Anita said that their relationship never went anywhere because he worked long hours and when he got promoted, he moved to his company's London office.

Anita got more involved in her sorority and still continued to run with the health club group. At one of the runs, she noticed Don, who was a new member of the group. He had joined the group near the holidays, when they had planned to get together for a party. When Don came to the holiday party, he mingled with everyone. Anita and he wound up standing next to each other and began talking. According to Anita, the conversation was about running, but she also discovered that he had grown up near her and they knew several of the same people. From that conversation, they got to know each other better when they would meet up to run. Anita said that their relationship started out very casually, without any expectations on her part. "Basically, I just thought he was a nice person and maybe someone who would become a friend. I can't say that I was looking for a man at this point because between my job, sorority and other volunteer commitments, I had a lot going on."

Don agreed with Anita's assessment, noting that "essentially we were in the same place in our lives—middle 20s, trying to find our way in life after college."

Anita also admitted that while she didn't think much about it, she hadn't really considered dating a white man. "I felt a little uneasy about it, not so much for me, but because I knew my parents would prefer me finding a black man. Also, I wondered how a white man would fit in with my black friends; how would this work? What about his family and friends? If my parents could have waved a magic wand, they would have found a professional black man for me. The problem was that even if I agreed with them, I didn't know any other than the guy who moved to London…and I can't say I felt that great an attraction to him. He was a nice guy, but always in the back of my mind, I didn't think I was really his type. I would not be surprised if he preferred other women of color or a white woman."

Don and Anita's relationship changed when she decided to attend her company's holiday party the following year. Not wanting to go to this event by herself, she asked Don if he would mind going with her. He agreed to go and the two of them had a good time. While Anita admitted to feeling a little awkward and self-conscious at first, she gradually got over this because "no one seemed to be paying any particular attention to us. Everyone appeared to be enjoying themselves…so I did, too."

For his part, Don said that when he saw Anita all dressed up (as opposed to being in her usual running or work-out clothes), "he was struck with how pretty she was." He noticed other men looking at her at the party, "and I was glad she was with me." After the party ended, Anita and he decided to have a drink at a bar before going home. Anita said that they rehashed the party and wound down. When Don reached Anita's apartment, he leaned over and gave her a 'goodnight' kiss before she got out of his car.

Anita recalled being surprised by Don's kiss, but later thought, *Hey, that felt pretty good.* When Don called her the next day, she could feel herself warming up to him. From that point, they began to see each other more frequently, outside of the health club and running, and over time, began to date in earnest.

Don said that "dating Anita grew to feel just natural. We got along well, we both liked doing the same things, and we thought alike on several issues. It was kind of funny when we went back to our parents' homes, how close we had grown up to each other."

Anita thinks that because she wasn't actively looking for a relationship, she found one. She said that while her parents weren't 'thrilled' Don was white, when they met and interacted with him a few times, they recognized that he was more like them than they would have ever imagined, and their misgivings began to crumble. According to Anita, "Don went from being this white boy I had found to being someone they enjoyed having around. He fit in well with my family; my brother, too. When we had children, my parents were happy to be grandparents."

Don's family had fewer initial reservations about their relationship than Anita's. Don's mother was interested in getting to know Anita from the time she realized that Don was serious about her. Don said his mother only mentioned once if he had thought of how his life might change marrying a black woman. "She said, 'You know, you may experience some problems you haven't had to deal with before, but then again, times have changed, and you two may be just fine.'" His father "just wanted to make certain I was 100% positive about my decision to marry Anita. He didn't want me to end up divorced as he had. I think he would have asked me virtually the same thing even if Anita were white. When I thought about it, I realized why Mom and Dad were concerned. After all, I hadn't dated that much, never had any serious long-term relationships before Anita, and now when I tell them I am getting married, I am marrying someone from a different race. Honestly, wouldn't most parents be concerned about that?"

When I asked Don and Anita if they had experienced any problems as an interracial couple, Don responded that "other than the random person on the street who may stare at us a little too long to be polite, no, not really." They both agreed that living where they do, interracial couples are not rare, even though most of these couples are black men with white women.

Asked if they had any advice for other people thinking about an interracial relationship, Anita responded, "If you have a lot in common, race is not going to matter in the long run; in the short term, there may be some adjustment issues, but when you love your spouse, you will just make the adjustments and move on."

ROSLYN AND EUGENE

Eugene and Roslyn have been married for twelve years and have two children. Eugene is in his early 40s and Roslyn is in her 30s. They met after Roslyn had graduated from college and moved to Washington D.C. to start a new job. She lived in an apartment with three other young women. One of these women was a college friend of Eugene's, originally from Jamaica. She convinced Roslyn to take a Spring vacation with her to Palm Beach, Florida.

Eugene was among the group of Roslyn's roommate's friends who agreed to meet in Florida at the same time. According to Eugene, Roslyn spent the first couple of days of the vacation "not really talking to anyone…probably because she was taking it all in" (the large number of people who were all alumni of the same college). Roslyn responded that she… "had two roommates who were white, even one from Texas," so she took her time feeling people out. Living in the apartment with three other women, she had heard a few remarks from some of their friends which were not appropriate.

Apparently Eugene sensed that Roslyn was not feeling comfortable in the group so he sought her out. Roslyn described Eugene as being "hilarious…he is just so funny sometimes. There was an instant warmth about him; he was so kind, it was great." By the time the vacation ended, they had exchanged phone numbers. Roslyn went back to Washington, D.C., and Eugene went back to Chicago.

A few days after he was home, he gave Roslyn a call. He had a work trip scheduled for Washington, D.C. a month later and wanted to get together again. Roslyn was initially hesitant about introducing Eugene to her friends because she knew they were very protective of her. Roslyn described Eugene to her friends as: "Well, he's 30, great, white and balding. And of course, they went, what? What did you say he is?" Once her friends met and hung out with the two of them, the conversation changed. They all thought Eugene was great. A few months later, Roslyn got a call from an Illinois senator candidate campaign's office to find out if she was interested in working for them. She wanted to believe that this was just a coincidence, but wondered how much Eugene, who is from a very politically active family, had to do with the job offer. No matter, Roslyn decided to take the position, which meant she had to move to Chicago. Even though the campaign had secured housing for Roslyn, she would have to live with three roommates and after living in that situation in D.C. she wanted to live on her own. Recognizing that she didn't know Chicago well enough to determine the best neighborhoods in which to reside, she asked Eugene if she could just "crash with him for a while. And Eugene was like, 'Yeah. Sure you can crash with me for a little.' And it was supposed to be only for a little while. But it turned into forever."

Roslyn told her mother over five phone calls about her plans to move to Chicago, what she was going to be doing, and who she would be living with. Her mother's response was, "Explain this to me" and for Roslyn and Eugene to come see her in Texas as soon as possible. Roslyn and Eugene went to Texas on their first free weekend. I asked Eugene if the initial meeting with Roslyn's mother went well, to which he responded, "No. Her mom forgot to put her tooth in, which had recently been knocked out. Be sure you put this in your book." Eugene found this to be funny since he, too, had dentures at the time. He had lost a few teeth while playing hockey. Roslyn's mother was very direct with them, inquiring when they were getting married. She would never approve of her daughter living with a "thirty-year-old balding white man" otherwise.

Roslyn's mother had taken the time to Google Eugene before he met her and had a favorable opinion of him, which made it easier to win her over. Roslyn's father, on the other hand, was not so impressed. According to Eugene, "he purposefully gave me a hard time." Her father was not into his daughter dating a white man.

Roslyn recalled that as a teenager, her parents had her participate in a cotillion. At the time, she had a white boyfriend, but her
father was very clear that he wasn't going to have his daughter be the
only participant escorted by a white guy. Roslyn remembered that
her father "didn't want people to know I would even date a white
guy."

Eugene recounted that Roslyn's father and uncle took him to a
little bar where they both "grilled him."

Later, they decided that they were going to engage Eugene in
some "hood stuff" in an attempt to intimidate him. Eugene noted,
"They failed miserably because I was prepared for them." On a
visit to Roslyn's brother's home, Eugene and she agreed to a game
of spades with her father and brother. Eugene had learned how to
play spades years earlier and "the two of us just destroyed them." Her
father continued trying to intimidate Eugene, throwing cards at him,
telling him he was going to take the car and leave them at his son's
home—anything to get a reaction.

Eugene responded, "'Well, it's my car, sir,' to which her father
said, 'Darn it, I don't care. Give me the keys.' And I said, 'No, not
doing that.'"

I asked Eugene what attracted him to Roslyn. He responded,
"Oh, a hot 22-year-old. Pretty simple." Also, Eugene stated, "Roslyn
was pretty fearless, willing to try anything." He recalled a story from
earlier in their relationship of how she wasn't scared to go canoeing
in a river known to be full of alligators. On another occasion, they
took a lion safari tour where you got to drive your car through a lion
habitat. Eugene didn't realize he didn't have much gas left in his tank

until they were about halfway through the enclosure. The other people in the car were very worried that they were going to be stuck in the habitat, but Roslyn thought the whole thing was funny.

Roslyn and Eugene lived together for nine years before they got married. When I asked if they had experienced any negative racial incidents since the time they have been together, they detailed three events from their years in Florida. One time when they tried to rent a house and had paid the security deposit, the realtor was told that the house had already been rented by another realtor but not taken off the MLS listing. Roslyn thought that because the house was in a predominantly Jewish neighborhood and the neighbors had seen her looking at it that it was suspicious Eugene and she weren't able to rent it. Second, one time the two of them went to a popular restaurant with communal seating. The restaurant was very crowded and they had to wait for about an hour before the hostess was able to seat them. Once they were seated, another couple left after finishing their dinner, leaving two open spaces at their table. Despite seating being at a premium, every time the hostess brought other patrons over to their table to sit next to them, they would refuse, preferring to wait for another open table. Roslyn recalls seeing how frustrated the hostess became each time white customers refused to sit at their table. Roslyn stated... "She [the hostess] kept apologizing and was so embarrassed, nobody will sit here, sort of shocked."

Eugene recounted a time when he played for a semi-pro football team just for fun. He knew the head coach and was one of the few centers. He played in most games during the first season. The next season, there was a change in coaching staff. Once during a practice Roslyn had to go to the field to see Eugene. One of the newer black coaches saw Roslyn and according to Eugene, "none of the other coaches had any problem with me dating a black woman at all. But I think this coach did. …I had a really hard time getting on the field after that. Even when some of the other linemen were screaming at him [the coach] to put me in, he wouldn't put me in. Now, in all fairness, the coach played another white guy, a tackle, the entire season and he didn't have a problem. And he was a great player. And the guys that played in front of me were very talented football players. So I don't want to take anything away from them. But it was definitely difficult. I had started a whole bunch of games in a row, and then the coach saw Roslyn and I was done. I was barely on the field, even as a reserve."

I asked Eugene and Roslyn if there was any advice they would give other couples planning to marry interracially. Eugene responded, "One thing you need to think about is that if you have children they are going to be black. And the difference—the cultural jump—I mean for your kids; there are people who will view your children in a certain way. And there's more racism out there than I thought there was, and so that may be something you have to deal with."

ANNE AND FRANK

Anne and Frank have been married for twenty years. They met while teaching at the same high school. Anne is seven years older than Frank and had been married previously to a black man for many years, by whom she had two daughters and two grandchildren. This is Frank's first marriage, and Anne and he are raising her two grandchildren.

I started the interview by asking if they had encountered any problems being an interracial couple.

Anne responded first by noting that her white mother-in-law initially had trouble with their relationship for several reasons. "First, I was older than her son by several years, had been married previously with children, and practiced a different religion than she did. She was not keen on her son taking on all of this responsibility with an older woman."

Frank acknowledged that his wife was telling the truth, but noted "once my mother got to know Anne better, it was interesting to see how she began to actually like her much better than his brother's wife, who was her favorite daughter-in-law at first."

I asked what brought about the change. Frank responded, "Anne is actually more sensitive to my mother's needs. When she (his mother) became sick with a serious illness, Anne jumped right in to help her without being asked. She would go to the store for her, bring her food so she didn't have to cook, and generally, just made certain that she didn't feel alone." Anne added that she didn't think what she did was any big deal. "Hey, I used to take care of my own mother, too, when she needed help. That was the way I was raised. When a family member needs help, you pitch in."

Frank's brother and sister-in-law were also supportive during that time, but their schedules were far more constrained.

Anne remarked that during the time she spent with her mother-in-law, they had an opportunity to talk about life in ways they hadn't previously. They discovered that they shared the same views on so many issues despite the generational and racial differences. Some months later, Anne heard from one of Frank's cousins that her mother-in-law had referred to her "as my favorite daughter-in-law" at a family dinner.

Referring to what attracted them to each other when they first met, Frank stated, "When I first saw Anne, I thought to myself, *Now that's a pretty woman.* I also liked what I saw of her personality…her kind way of speaking to the other teachers and staff, and her students seemed to like and respect her, too. You know, when high school kids like a teacher, that person has done something that they admire."

Frank said that it was easy to approach Anne because it seemed they were always in the cafeteria or at the copy machine at the same time, and would often sit next to each other at faculty meetings. Their relationship developed slowly and casually over a few months. Once, when a faculty meeting had ended, he asked Anne if she would like to go out for coffee at Starbucks afterwards. This became a pattern and from then on they started going out to dinner from time to time.

Frank stated, "I wasn't looking for a relationship when we started dating, but as I got to know her, I came to realize that she was becoming an important person in my life."

Anne agreed with Frank and mentioned that she "appreciated that Frank would ask me out, but my priority when we met was my two children."

When I asked Anne how her family felt about her dating Frank, she responded that she didn't tell them for several months because they knew she had been through a tough divorce years earlier, and she wasn't certain their relationship was going to be serious, especially with the age difference. Interestingly, Anne was not as concerned about Frank's race as she was his age. According to Anne, "really, how likely is it that a much younger man wants to marry an older woman with kids? Yeah, sure I thought about race, but I thought the age difference and kids would be the deal breaker."

Anne started taking the relationship seriously when Frank asked her to be his date at a special charity fundraising event. She knew several of his longtime friends would be in attendance. As she said, "This was his first social acknowledgement to his friends about our relationship." Anne noted, "I was the only black person at this event, but this didn't bother me in the least. Frank was so attentive and made it plain to everyone that we were a couple."

Eventually, Anne introduced Frank to her mother and sister. (Her father was deceased.) While they thought "he was a nice guy… my mother reminded me 'not to get too involved with him' because she didn't see him taking on all of my baggage." Her sister was more enthusiastic, noting that Frank "had something about him that made her think he just might be the one." Further, her sister remarked, "Why not try something different? You already had enough bad experience with John [Anne's former husband]."

Anne and Frank dated for about three years before he asked her to marry him. According to Anne, "We got to know each other well, saw how we functioned together as a couple, and went to counseling to make certain I didn't bring to this marriage any negative behaviors or attitudes from my previous one." Frank observed that he "was impressed that Anne considered as many aspects as possible before agreeing to marry him. She thought of situations that I would not have considered to get my opinion on how I would handle them. I think we were as prepared as any two people could be when we got married. You might be surprised to know that of all the situations we discussed, our racial difference was one of the least important; not that it was unimportant, but becoming a stepfather without having any previous parenting experience and dealing with Anne's former husband (who even though he didn't have custody still didn't like it that she was marrying a white man) were more compelling issues."

Fifteen years into their marriage, Anne was faced with the decision of taking in her two grandchildren after her daughter's marriage ended. Her daughter needed to return to school for additional training to attain a sustainable career. Her former husband was minimally employed and had an unstable lifestyle. Not wanting to see her grandchildren suffer the effects of living in an unsuitable environment with two unstable parents, Anne and Frank agreed to have the grandchildren live with them.

Anne is grateful that Frank didn't hesitate to take in her grandchildren and noted he provides the kind of male role modeling they needed to experience. He treats them the same way he treated her children, and she thinks that this is one reason why her daughter recognized she needed to leave her husband. "She remembered how Frank always treated her and when her husband didn't treat her the same way, she knew something was wrong."

For his part Frank says that "Anne's children were the only children I was ever going to have, so it is the same with her grandchildren. We have a good life together; we can manage this situation, too. The important thing is that everyone be prepared to take care of themselves one day." Anne and Frank expect to be the primary parents for her grandchildren for about three more years—the time it should take for her daughter to complete her training and get employed.

As Anne noted, "at the end of these four years, Frank and I will still be able to do some of the things we would do if we didn't have children around." Frank added, "Fortunately, we are used to kids and teenagers so this isn't as big an adjustment as it might be for some other couples."

TONI AND RICHARD

Toni is forty-five years old and Richard is forty-seven. Toni started the interview by noting that she had grown up in Alabama and was raised by her great-grandparents. Her mother was not married when she became pregnant, so she gave Toni up to be raised by her great-grandparents while she completed school. Several years later, Toni's mother met her current husband, by whom she has a second daughter.

Toni stated that her great grandparents were very religious (Baptist) and strict. She dated infrequently, and the young men she dated were always black. She didn't know many white people growing up, having little association with them. She graduated from high school and started college at the University of Alabama, where she didn't do well academically. She moved to Birmingham, Alabama, where she worked part-time and went back to college, completing a degree in finance.

Toni noted that one of her goals was to leave Alabama so ten years after completing her bachelor's degree she moved to the Chicago area and lived with one of her uncles. It was while living in Chicago that she met her husband. They met on BlackPlanet.com, a dating site for black people.

Toni related that Richard had joined BlackPlanet to intentionally meet black women. When Richard contacted her, she didn't have any idea that he was white. They began to chat for several weeks before she agreed to meet him in person. This was when he told her that he had a confession to make—he wasn't black; he was Irish. Toni stated, "At first, I was angry that he had deceived me and told him that if he had deceived me about his race, how would I know he wouldn't lie to me about anything else?" Richard asked her to give him another chance; after all, she had been interested in him when she thought he was black. Toni reluctantly agreed to at least meet him in person, but when it came time for her to show up at the restaurant they had chosen, she backed out. Richard then sent her an email, "and it was the sweetest email, you know. I can't remember the exact wording but it was basically, I'd really like to meet you. You seem nice…just give me a chance. If you don't like me, you haven't lost anything." Toni stated the email made her feel bad she had ditched him so once again they rescheduled another restaurant at which to meet.

The second time Toni agreed to meet Richard wound up being a pretty cold Chicago day. She got lost on the way to the restaurant, and when she finally found it, she had difficulty parking. Toni admits to "not being in the best of moods" when she approached the restaurant. However, much to her surprise, when she saw Richard, "I thought, he looks adorable. He's got on this black hat and a black trench coat…and he's standing out there and very much a gentle-man. Of course, I was shaking like a leaf."

When I asked why, Toni responded, "I was scared, you know. I mean, I had never gone out with a white guy before. Thinking back on it now, it sounds a little stupid, I guess, but you know, I just didn't know what to expect. He was very nice, and we had a great conversation over dinner. I don't know why I thought going out with a white guy would be different from going out with a black guy, probably because I grew up in Alabama."

Within about a week of their first date, Richard asked Toni to go out with him again. They did and this time she remembers being bothered that Richard was a little shorter than she is and a little over-weight. Toni said she had never dated anyone shorter than she was because she loved wearing heels. However, after a few more dates with Richard where they continued to have a good time together, she chided herself, noting that "if the only reason I stop dating him is because of his height and weight, I sound a little superficial."

Toni said she liked everything else about Richard; he was a nice guy, he had a great job, he had a great personality, and he gave her a lot of attention. Why would she stop dating him?

Toni and Richard continued to date for a few months when he asked her if she would like to meet his family. His father was deceased but his mother, brother and grandmother lived in Ohio. Toni recalled that Richard's mother was very nice to her but was a quiet person, which made her uncomfortable. Toni is very talkative and quiet people make her nervous. Richard's brother was also a nice person and very accepting of her. She learned later that Richard's family was used to his dating black women or other women of color so meeting her was no big deal for them. Toni asked Richard why he preferred black women and if he had ever been in a serious relationship with a white woman. He responded that "he had but, generally, he found black women more interesting than white women. He had a white girlfriend once who was a nice person, but basically he found her boring."

On the other hand, Richard warned Toni that his grandmother was not accepting of his relationships with black women and made disparaging remarks about them, calling one of them 'darkie'. Toni responded, "You know if your grandmother says that to me, I'm going to go off on her, right? And he was like, 'Oh, she won't say that'...and maybe needless to say, on that trip, I didn't meet his grandmother."

Toni's mother didn't meet Richard until after they had married, but her uncle did meet him. According to Toni, her uncle "pretty much accepted Richard right from the beginning after having a few conversations with him. He didn't find it unusual that a white guy would be attracted to me, but then again he didn't think like the people back in Alabama." Her mother was surprised that Toni had decided to marry a white man but, "since she didn't raise me, and I was older than she was when she got married, she didn't try to discourage me from doing this either."

By the time Toni and Richard had been together for ten months, she wanted to go on vacation. Richard agreed to go with her, but wanted them to go to Paris. At the top of the Eiffel Tower, Richard surprised Toni by proposing to her. Toni was shocked because she hadn't thought about marrying him and always believed you should date someone for at least a couple of years before deciding to get engaged. She recalled how the crowd surrounding them at the Eiffel Tower observed Richard proposing to her and shouted out cheers and good wishes. Caught up in the romance of the situation, Toni accepted Richard's proposal and a year later they married. They lived together for about six months before their wedding, which took place at the Paris hotel in Las Vegas, "because Richard wanted to keep that French theme going."

At the wedding, Toni's uncle walked her down the aisle, one of her cousins was a bridesmaid and Richard's brother was his best man. Both of their families were in attendance and everyone got along well. Even Richard's grandmother attended the wedding and when she met Toni, "while she wasn't warm and friendly, she was at least pleasant." Toni remembers her wedding and reception as being one of the happiest days of her life.

The only person who had a problem with her marriage to Richard was her stepfather, who she didn't know all that well and whose opinion she would not have considered important. He refused to come to the wedding and told Toni that if they came to Alabama to visit her mother they could not stay at their home. Toni said, "He only objected to me marrying Richard because he was white. He couldn't say another thing against him, only that he didn't like me marrying a white man." Toni didn't find this surprising because her stepfather didn't associate with white people and he lived in a segregated black community in Alabama.

Toni and Richard were married for seven years before their relationship ended in divorce, the reasons for which will be discussed in the next section.

CLARICE AND ROBERT

Clarice is sixty-five years old and her husband Robert is seventy-eight. They have been married for thirty years. Clarice started our interview by noting that she met her husband when she was eighteen. At the time, she had just completed high school in Texas and had embarked on a modeling career. While auditioning for modeling work, she applied for part-time secretarial work at an insurance company. Robert was her supervisor.

Clarice noted that she was a model until around the age of twenty-seven, but still needed the additional income she earned working at the insurance company. When she felt her modeling career was coming to an end, she decided to open a beauty salon/day spa and needed a business loan. With no business background, she was turned down for a loan by a few banks. Becoming discouraged about her prospects, she confided her troubles to Robert. He agreed to loan Clarice the funds she needed with the caveat that he would be her business partner. He agreed also to manage the financial accounts for the business, as he had a degree in accounting.

The beauty salon/day spa grew to be very successful. Working so closely together, the two of them got to know each other well and recognized how compatible they were. Robert's career continued to grow as well at the insurance company, where he earned numerous promotions, resulting in his becoming quite wealthy. Clarice noted that as their respective careers grew, so too did their feelings for each other. Robert had been married briefly as a young man before she met him, but had no children. After his divorce, he had devoted himself to his career while taking care of his mother after his father died. Clarice stated that she knew she didn't want to have children so marrying Robert, who is thirteen years older than she is, didn't pose any problems for her.

I asked Clarice if either of their families had any racial concerns about their relationship, to which she replied, "No, no problems with his race, but my mother was concerned about the age difference. I think she kept hoping that I would change my mind about having children before it was too late. But by the time we married, I was already thirty-five and Robert was almost forty-eight—too old in my mind to start having children." Clarice was raised by a single mother and her father was not active in her life so she didn't seek out his opinion about Robert. Clarice added also that by the time Robert and she got married, "he was far too independent to care what anyone would think about us. He had been married before and knew what he was getting into, and his mother wasn't the kind of person to interfere with his life anyway."

Clarice further noted that Robert would not have cared what any of his other family members thought of their marriage because he wasn't close to anyone but his mother and brother, both of whom lived in other states. Clarice contended that Robert's family treated her fine; "the first couple of times we were together, I could tell they were uncomfortable, but I never picked up any hostility. I don't know if they would have treated me differently if I were white, but I believe it was more like they felt awkward because I just looked different from most other people they knew. So…I would say they were curious, but not hostile."

SANDRA AND JAMES

Sandra and James met when they were in the military. Sandra was in the Army and James was in the Navy and both were stationed in San Diego, California. The Army was in charge of inspecting the food service and supply on the Navy base and Sandra was often assigned this task. One day while completing her work, Sandra overheard James talking with some of his Navy buddies, wondering why the Army was responsible for food inspection. Sandra and her coworker didn't interject themselves into their conversation, continuing with their task. A week later, Sandra saw James at the commissary on base and spoke to him, letting him know that she had overheard his conversation musing on why the Army oversaw the inspection for the Navy. She started to fill him in on the details when he interrupted to inquire where she was from. When she responded Chicago, he laughed and told her that he was too. That exchange led to a more in-depth conversation and their friendship blossomed. When both of them returned to Chicago, they continued to date and eventually married four years after their first meeting. They have one daughter who is sixteen years old.

Sandra stated that she joined the Army right after high school, while James enlisted a few months later. After she graduated from college, she went into pharmaceutical sales and James pursued an advanced degree in counseling. James primarily works with low income minority teen males and has developed a good relationship with them. He never mentioned that his wife is African American, choosing not to trade on her ethnicity to gain favor.

One day, however, when Sandra had to meet James at work, the teens learned that she was black. They asked him later why he never told them, to which he responded that he wanted them to respect him for himself. James confided that once the teens knew about her, they developed a closer relationship with him.

Further, James remarked to Sandra that a few of the black women who worked at his site also became friendlier when they learned she was African American. He thought that his having a black wife made the women take more of an interest in him.

Sandra added that James and she didn't meet any opposition to their relationship from either family or friends. They have been married for twenty-four years and their only concern is to make certain that their daughter understands her biracial identity. James believes that too many biracial children are made to feel as if they have to choose sides when it comes to racial identity, and they want their daughter to understand that she belongs in both worlds.

BARBARA AND MARK

Barbara is sixty-four years old and she has been married to Mark, sixty-five, for fourteen years. Barbara met Mark through the dating service, It's Just Lunch. Barbara joined It's Just Lunch on the advice of two friends who had made successful romantic connections through the company.

Barbara put in her application that she was looking for some-one who had some life experience, a sense of humor, and a good heart. Based on her background, she indicated that she would like to meet someone who was comparably educated, but she didn't indi-cate any other physical, religious, or racial characteristics. When asked if looks mattered, she said no.

She was first set up with a 'Nigerian midget' who was charm-ing and took extra care in his dress to prepare for their meeting. However, a love connection wasn't in the cards because she realized she would not be comfortable with a man that much shorter than her. Next, she was set up with numerous other professional men from around the world, but after a few of these dates, she realized that she wanted to marry an American.

At the end of her contract with It's Just Lunch, a counselor called and told her about Mark. Barbara learned that he was recently divorced, and so she said no because she didn't think he would be emotionally available. The counselor convinced her that he was a sweet man, and that she really should meet him, and so she agreed.

The first meeting took place at a popular Chicago restaurant and she decided he was 'nice enough' but at the end of the meal, when he received the check he told her what she owed on the bill. She was surprised about this, even though the rules are that the first date is 'Dutch' because on all earlier dates the guy had insisted on paying for the full bill. Later in their relationship, Mark explained to her that he hadn't had any dating experience in twenty-three years and was just simply following the rules.

Barbara doesn't know what possessed her to go on a second date with Mark. She discovered that his deceased father and her deceased sister had the same birthday, which she took as a good omen. Their birthday wound up being her wedding date two years later.

I asked Barbara how race impacted their relationship. Did anyone object or raise this as an issue?

Barbara stated she was a little concerned about meeting Mark's family because they are from small-town Indiana, and his mother is first generation Italian. Dispelling her hesitation, Mark's mother was, in Barbara's words, "absolutely wonderful from their first meeting." Mark told Barbara that if his father were alive he knows he would have loved her, too. When one of Mark's brothers learned of their relationship he said, "You are the real trail blazer in the family." Mark responded, "Sounds like you are living in the 1950s" and just laughed.

When Mark's son found out about their relationship he told Barbara, "We were surprised [Mark was dating interracially] because most interracial relationships don't last." Barbara was taken aback at this statement but responded, "It depends on the social class and education of the couple." This shut his son up. Mark's younger daughter warmly took to Barbara while his older daughter remained distant, which Barbara attributes in part to other issues she had stemming from her mother's quick remarriage.

Mark and Barbara primarily lived in integrated communities for the first few years of their marriage, but for the past decade they have lived in predominantly white suburbs due to the proximity to their jobs. This is when Barbara and Mark began to have different experiences. Barbara noted that in the three positions she has held in these white communities, all of which she was overeducated and overqualified for, she has experienced micro-racist aggressions from white coworkers. She didn't endure this kind of behavior when she worked in Chicago.

According to Barbara, since the beginning of the Trump era, she has been feeling increasingly isolated in the suburb where Mark and she currently reside. She is hoping to move to a community where she believes the residents and she will have shared interests. In her former social circles, everyone was a Democrat; where she lives now, she is hesitant to get involved in the community because "you never know who you are going to offend." Barbara recalls telling Mark on their second date, "I don't care about race or religion, but if you are a Republican I don't think we will have a future." Mark laughs about that now because she was in an all-Democratic environment, and now they have to navigate around Republicans. At the time of their second date, Mark was supporting Ralph Nader.

Barbara noted that she was the only woman Mark dated other than his first wife. She doesn't believe her race was important to him. She recalled that he was intrigued by her background and he adored her stepfather. The two men formed a close bond. Barbara remembers that a couple of her previous white boyfriends also admired and respected her stepfather.

Her parents had no problems with any of the men she dated. They just wanted her to be happy. Barbara ended our interview by stating that even though it took her a long time to find "the one" she knows that Mark was worth the wait.

SUMMARY

The fourteen couples profiled in this chapter on black women married to white men present a wide range of experiences including the length of the marriages, the ages of the spouses, the circumstances under which these relationships began, and the factors which have allowed most of these marriages to thrive. It is important to note these couples recognized that to the degree race or racial concerns were a part of their relationships these issues needed to be addressed openly and honestly prior to getting married.

CHAPTER 6

BLACK WOMEN DIVORCED FROM WHITE MEN

The smallest category of black women interviewed for this book was those divorced from white husbands. Divorce under any condition is usually the result of multiple factors between a couple. I wanted to determine what, if any role race or racial issues played in the divorce.

It is also important to note here that several sources have indicated the divorce rate for couples comprised of a black wife and a white husband is far *lower* than the rate for couples comprised of a black husband and a white wife. (14) Moreover, one study by the National Council on Family Relations found that black women with white husbands are nearly forty-four percent *less likely* to divorce than couples in which both partners are white. (15)

EUNICE

Eunice met her former husband, Michael, at an elite private liberal arts college on the East Coast. She said it was easy for her to be attracted to him because "he was funny. He was just so engaging. He had this, I don't know, ability to like command attention from everyone in the room because he just like had so much to say and was just such a wonderful person." They met when they were freshman, but didn't start dating until their junior year when she was between nineteen and twenty years old. By the time of their divorce, they had been together for thirteen years, even though they were married for about four years.

Eunice noted that her relationship with Michael was exclusive 'right from the beginning.' They took a class together and their social circles overlapped. Neither of them dated anyone else while in college.

After graduation, Eunice wanted to travel because she hadn't done any study abroad programs as an undergraduate. She wound up moving to Japan to teach English as a Second Language for a year. Michael decided to start a PhD program and they had a long distance monogamous relationship where they spoke often but only saw each other once during that time. According to Eunice, Michael and she were "serious people and serious about each other." Besides, she "is not the type of person who can have multiple partners. Even the idea seemed foreign to me."

When Eunice returned to the U.S., Michael and she moved in together. They lived in Boston where Michael was in graduate school. Once she decided to attend graduate school in the Midwest, they were faced with having a long distance relationship again. This time, however, they saw each other often, traveling back and forth between the two cities. After two years, Eunice received a fellowship which allowed her to move to Canada for a year. Michael moved with her.

I asked Eunice if Michael's race was ever a problem for her. She responded, "No, when I saw Michael, I saw someone who I thought of as Latino, even though he looked white. It was interesting meeting his family being like, wait a second, you're actually completely German and Czech." (Michael's mother is from Ecuador).

Eunice's parents didn't have any problems with Michael's race either. Reflecting on how her parents thought about Michael she noted, "I actually think he was less threatening to my family than if I had brought home a black man because I think they saw us as being friends and having a great friendship. And I think, especially with my dad, if I had brought home a black man…that he would have read it in a more sexual way than two friends coming together, which is how a lot of people, you know, interpreted Michael and me."

Michael's parents also liked and accepted Eunice right away. As she recalls, "Over the course of thirteen years that we were together, I spent probably eight Christmases with his family." Moreover, when Eunice's parents divorced, her father would spend Christmas with Michael's family as well. As Eunice stated, "All of us saw each other on a regular basis."

I asked Eunice how her mother felt about Michael. Eunice responded, "I know she liked him. I don't think he would have been the one that my mom would have chosen for me, whereas I know my dad and he got along so well. They were such close friends, and I know it's been very painful for my dad to kind of leave that friendship. As for my mom, I think she was very accepting, and, you know, at the end of the day just wanted someone who cared about me. And she could tell that Michael really cared and loved me. That was the most important thing to her."

Eunice further stated that the divorce was hard on her since she was very close to Michael's mother and sister.

I asked Eunice if Michael and she had run into any problems as an interracial couple. She replied that during their marriage they lived in St. Louis where they felt a lot of racial tension. "Michael was called a nigger lover in public, which was very hurtful…and you know, there were some people who were just plain mean to us. I had befriended some black women who began to treat me very differently when they found out that Michael was white. I feel like that changed our relationship or the way they perceived me in certain ways, but it was never verbalized."

Eunice recalls that many people simply didn't assume Michael and she were a couple. "Many times in stores, people would refer to us separately." Further illustrating her point, Eunice recounted a particularly funny story. "One time, we went out for drinks with a friend of a friend. And that friend found out Michael and I were living together and said something along the lines of 'oh, so how do you guys do that? How are you doing that in a one bedroom place? Do you like have separate beds and are like living in the same space?'"

Compounding the problem is that Eunice is tall and slender and Michael is tall but even thinner than she is. Eunice thought when people saw them together "that combined with the difference in our race, this might have been a somewhat jarring visual combination for some people."

Analyzing her marriage from the perspective of having been divorced for nearly five years, Eunice believes that the marriage was a "good part of my life."

So what caused them to divorce? Eunice paused before giving her response. She noted that for both of them, they were each other's first serious relationship and the first people either of them dated outside of their racial group. They were very attracted to each other and in some ways she believed she just "fell into the relationship with him." Eunice recalled, "He was just so engaging. He had this, I don't know, ability to like command attention from everyone in the room because he just had so much to say and was just such a wonderful person."

Over the time they were married, Eunice began to feel uncomfortable about their relationship. One of her main anxieties was what would happen if they had children. She noted, "I don't think I was concerned about them being biracial. I think I was most concerned about them not being identifiably black, because I am a very fair-skinned black woman. And you know, there is societal baggage that can be put on black people that look white basically."

Eunice then brought up another reason for their divorce, undoubtedly the most important one. During their marriage, when both of them were completing their doctorates, it was not uncommon for Michael's parents to help them financially. Initially this did not bother Eunice but, when the financial support continued beyond graduate school, she realized that she was not comfortable accepting their money. Michael was not concerned about receiving money from his parents; he believed that they were happy to help get them on their feet financially. Eunice observed that she came from a family where "it was expected you worked hard for what you got, and I would never have viewed my parents as a source of income once I had completed school, even if they had offered." Their differing financial views became a source of tension in their relationship. It was further exacerbated by the fact that Eunice worked with black men who she said "worked very hard for every cent they made" and she knew they would not have the same opportunities that Michael had. Recognizing the differences between them, she stated, "How would I describe it? Sort of an economic entitlement that I feel he had because of his whiteness that I do not have because of my blackness in this country. And that did play a very, very, huge role. And when we divorced, I lost some of my privilege to a certain extent."

I asked Eunice what advice she would give young black women about dating interracially. She responded, "I would just tell them everyone is an individual and to stop thinking within racial boxes. Everyone comes with certain baggage or ideas or whatever, but a date is a date between two people, just as a relationship is. Don't get caught up in too much racial stuff because at the end of the day it is all exterior stuff."

Postscript on Eunice: After her divorce she moved to another city where she is currently teaching and in a serious relationship with an African man.

SHEILA

I met Sheila and her husband fifteen years ago when I interviewed them for my first book on interracially married couples. Her husband and she were in their early thirties, employed in the same profession as writers for a major newspaper, and the parents of a young son. I learned through a mutual friend that the couple had divorced about five years after we had met so I wanted to know if race or racial concerns had anything to do with their divorce. When I questioned Sheila, she immediately responded, "No, I can honestly say that race had nothing to do with our divorce. The two main reasons for the divorce were personality and lifestyle differences. You know, nowadays it is hard to stay married to anyone."

Sheila then continued our conversation by telling me that the marriage had lasted for ten years even though they were separated for about five years before the divorce. When they separated, they were in no hurry to get divorced, in part because of their son, who they continued to raise together. However, sometime after their separation, her husband began a relationship with another black woman. When the woman became pregnant and gave birth to their child, he wanted to finally get divorced from Sheila so he could remarry.

For her part, after Sheila separated from her husband, she began to date again. Her next serious relationship, which lasted for about six and a half years, was with a black man. Currently, she is involved in another relationship with a black man with whom she went to high school. She noted that she found him on Facebook and they started talking. When they were in high school, they didn't really know each other that well. The relationship has been going on for a little more than a year, but is long distance. This poses its challenges but Sheila is confident that if it becomes more serious they will work through the long distance issue. I asked Sheila if she had purposely sought out relationships with black men after her divorce. She responded, "No, not at all. It just worked out that way. If this relationship doesn't work out, I would still be open to dating outside of the race."

Postscript on Sheila: She continues to run her own media company and is working as a ghostwriter. Her former husband and she continue to co-parent their son.

TONI

Toni is the woman who was married to Richard for six years and whose story was detailed in the section on black women married to white men. Toni met Richard through an online dating website focused on black people. Richard pursued Toni and about two and a half years after they met, they married. When I asked Toni why they wound up getting divorced, she replied, "Once we were married, I started to notice things I hadn't noticed before. Not that he changed, it was just I started seeing who Richard really was."

According to Toni, even though she knew Richard was in politics, she hadn't realized just how much time he spent involved in politics. In retrospect, she met Richard during an off election year which was why he had so much time to date her. Once they married, the actual time they spent together began to rapidly diminish.

As Toni recalled, "Within a few months of our marriage, he gets a promotion on his job to a big position, and so all of his time was spent either doing politics or doing work. And I'll never forget, it was an election year; it was his election. And I'm sitting at home by myself and he left at like 6:00 a.m., before I got up. He comes home and I'm having dinner by myself, which was a sore spot with me because when I lived in Birmingham, Alabama, I always ate by myself. When I moved to Illinois, I ate with my uncle. And it felt good not to have to eat alone. So I'm sitting, having dinner by myself, drinking a glass of wine and thinking. Richard sees me and says something along the lines of 'when this election is over, blah, blah, blah' and walks out the door. I remember picking up my wine glass and just throwing it at the door, which was dumb because I had to clean it up. I was just so angry. I was that fed up, you know. Election processes—I don't know if people realize it or not, when somebody's running in an election, that's months out of your life. It seems to go on forever."

Toni said that Richard considered himself trying to compromise by taking her to the Dominican Republic for her 40th birthday. However, once there, he continued to work on the election back home, spending little time with her. Their sex life suffered because there was no time for intimacy.

The conversation which added to the end of their marriage came about three years into their relationship when Richard admitted to Toni that he actually didn't want to have any children. Toni was shocked by his confession because before they married, they had discussed having children, even going so far as to pick out names they would give them. Richard told Toni that he realized if she were upset about how much time he spent away from home, it wouldn't be any better for the children.

Toni said she tried to keep the relationship together for a couple more years because she felt getting a divorce represented a failure, a character flaw. She tried to become more involved in politics with him, which he appreciated, but she realized that being a politician's wife was not for her. In the end, Toni said that Richard's inability to sustain a work-life balance was the major cause of their divorce. It was Richard who filed for the divorce because toward the end they were not speaking even during the little time they actually saw each other. Toni laughed bitterly at the irony of Richard sending her an email letting her know he had filed for divorce and what his attorney thought the divorce would cost. To keep matters simple, they agreed to walk away from the marriage with what they had each brought to it.

Postscript on Toni: During her divorce from Richard, she connected with a black man she had known while living in Birmingham, Alabama but who was married then. Turns out he was going through a divorce, too. They were each other's 'sounding board' through their respective divorces and their initial friendship became romantic. He moved to Chicago and they married a few years later. Interestingly enough, her husband met Richard and the two of them became friendly working on a political campaign. It is not uncommon for the three of them to have dinner together since Richard has not remarried.

GEORGIA

Georgia and Mario met in law school and dated for six years prior to their marriage. They were married for twenty years before they divorced and have two teenage children. Georgia stated that race was not an integral part of their divorce, but as the marriage deteriorated, cultural expectations certainly were. These cultural differences had not come up during the early years of their marriage.

Over the course of their relationship, while both were employed as attorneys, Georgia had the more financially successful career.

Georgia grew up with the expectation that she would always have a career; "after all, why spend the time acquiring a law degree and not use it?" After their children were born, Mario became resentful about her career even though he didn't make as much money as she did and they needed her income.

When they finally went to counseling, it came out that Mario really wanted Georgia to be a housewife, something he never articulated before they got married. The combination of her earning more money than he was and not being willing to assume a more traditional wife and mother role made their marriage difficult. According to Georgia, "Mario became more confrontational and resented the time I spent away from home." Moreover, Mario hated that she participated in Jack and Jill, a black social organization designed to allow black children living in predominantly white suburban areas to get to know each other.

As the tension escalated in their home, Georgia filed for divorce. Their divorce was final in October 2015 and neither have remarried. Georgia indicated that she spends as little time as necessary communicating with Mario, and only does so because they co-parent their children. Mario accused Georgia of having an affair while they were married, which Georgia vehemently denied.

I asked Georgia if she has a relationship with any of Mario's family since the divorce. She replied that his parents are deceased and she was close to one of Mario's two sisters. While this relationship has become strained, her former sisters-in-law still include her children in family activities. Her children remain very close to their paternal cousins.

I asked Georgia if she had any advice for other black women who were dating white men. She responded, "While it is probably easier to date inside the race, each person is different. The main thing would be to have someone in your life who will support you and your career."

Georgia then added that she had dated black men prior to her marriage to Mario. However, she felt that "every black man I met who had it all together was arrogant…not particularly kind or caring. I didn't want to deal with that attitude."

Postscript on Georgia: While she hasn't met anyone special so far, she realizes that it is going to take some time. She is open to dating men from any racial/ethnic group.

NANCY

Nancy and Don were married for sixteen years prior to their divorce. Nancy comes from a prominent political family, while Don's parents were academics. Don is Jewish and Nancy is Catholic. Nancy and Don met in college when both were involved in a political campaign. They soon realized they shared the same political views and wanted to continue participating in politics once they graduated. They married three years after graduation and eventually had two children while living on the East Coast.

Their families were accepting of their relationship despite the racial and religious differences. The strain on their marriage began when they decided to pursue different careers. Don applied and was accepted into a prestigious psychology graduate program in the Midwest while Nancy became more involved in the political life of her family. In order for Don to take advantage of the graduate program, they would need to move from the East Coast. Not wanting to give up his opportunity, Nancy and Don initially agreed to move together with their children.

However, after about six months living in the new location, Nancy realized that she was not able to progress in her career long distance. Even with the help of her in-laws, who lived nearby and offered to help take care of the children, Nancy recognized that by "being so physically far away from where the action was taking place", her role was diminished.

Within a year of moving from the East Coast, Nancy moved back alone. Don and she agreed to try a commuter marriage until he could move back to the East Coast with her. The children stayed with their grandparents and Nancy arranged to return to see them often. She appreciated the stability her in-laws generously provided their grandchildren, allowing Don and her to progress in their respective careers. This arrangement worked well for about five years, until Don was offered a prestigious fellowship in Europe after receiving his PhD. Since they had lived apart while Don was in graduate school, Nancy counted on their family being reunited on the East Coast after he was finished as originally planned.

Don agreed to fulfill his promise and along with their older child, the family moved back to the East Coast. The younger child remained with the grandparents in the Midwest because she wanted to finish high school where she had started.

The move back to the East Coast was the beginning of the end of their marriage. While Nancy was comfortable in her career, Don was not able to find a position which he enjoyed. He lamented giving up the European fellowship, which took a toll on their relationship. Recognizing that Don was unhappy, Nancy encouraged him to re-apply for the fellowship. Much to his surprise, Don received a second fellowship offer which he decided to accept after discussion with Nancy. After so many years spent living apart, and recognizing that accepting the fellowship meant the two of them would now be living a continent away from each other, and additionally that their children were nearly grown, Nancy and Don decided to divorce.

Their divorce was amicable and the two of them remain friends and co-parents. As Nancy stated, "We didn't realize when we got married that we would want different careers because we were too blinded by our youthful passions. It would not have been fair to either of us to give up what we each wanted."

Postscript on Nancy: Neither Don or she have remarried; both have dated sporadically and continue to see each other through their children.

LESLEY

Lesley is forty-five years old and has been divorced for six years. She was married for six years to Ted, who she describes as really a nerd. So how did this black woman journalist wind up married for six years to a nerd? Her story is as follows.

Lesley began by stating that she grew up at the edge of Detroit in a dysfunctional family. Her parents are divorced and she has four half-siblings from their second marriages. She described herself as 'thick' and even at her thinnest, "I am still a hardy girl." Growing up she was relentlessly teased by the black boys in her neighborhood, who called her several derogatory names based on her dark skin color. Lesley recalled, "There wasn't a day I went to school that one of these boys didn't call me a name...even one who is now famous for being a Chicago Bull."

Fortunately, she did well in school, eventually went to college and earned a degree in journalism. Her career began to take off and she lived all over the country before settling in the Chicago area. While working for a newspaper, she met her former husband, who worked there as well. During one after-work gathering at a downtown pub, the two of them were the last to leave. Lesley had been warned about Ted by other co-workers, who told her that he was a jerk and not very friendly. He told Lesley that he had overheard her talking about how much she liked to bike ride and that he did as well, so maybe they could take a ride together sometime.

Lesley took this initial overture as not meaning very much. After all, she had not dated many men and never thought a white man would be romantically interested in her. As she pointed out, "I hadn't even been able to attract a light-skinned black man, so why would I make the assumption that a white man would be interested in me?"

Lesley detailed the difficulty that dating black men posed for her. For example, once she met a black guy in Chicago who seemed to engage her in conversation every time they ran into each other at various events. "And he made a point one time of telling me that he probably would ask me out if I owned some Ferrigamo shoes. And I said, well, you know, if that's really something that's important to you, then you need to buy the women you take out Ferrigamo shoes." Lesley added that she seemed to meet other black men who were equally as obnoxious or superficial.

"So I consciously made up my mind that if I resumed my career in Chicago, I would have to sacrifice a dating life; black men just did not appreciate me physically in the way that the men in the South did. And the black men in the South, I didn't appreciate them because I didn't feel like they were bringing as much intellectually or economically to the table. So I thought it was a trade-off."

Lesley noted that her first bike riding date with Ted almost didn't happen. She had scheduled a hair appointment prior to their meeting time. However, the shop owner was running way behind that day and she ran late getting back home. Ted was just pulling off in his car when she reached her apartment building so she ran a block to get to him at the stop sign. He appreciated the effort she made to stop him.

They never made it bike riding that day but they did go to the 57th Street bookstore. They discovered they liked doing simple things together, such as reading The New York Times, and grew very comfortable being together without talking. As the relationship became more serious, they decided to move in together. Lesley told Ted that she wasn't going to live with him without some formal commitment. While she knew neither of them was ready to get married, she felt he needed to affirm their relationship. Ted bought her a beautiful sapphire and diamond ring.

They settled on living in Rogers Park because they both felt comfortable in this integrated neighborhood.

Ted took Lesley to meet his family, who were from downstate Illinois. Lesley remembers his parents, sister and grandmother being very nice to her. However, she later learned that his grandmother told Ted's father to tell him that "they didn't need to have any black people in their family." Her parents, stepparents and grandmother also met Ted. While they were friendly enough toward him, later her grandmother said, "I don't see this relationship lasting; it is too intellectual, no emotion." Lesley and Ted enjoyed a good laugh over their grandmothers' comments.

Ted and Lesley wound up living together for three years before they married. Things were going well for both of them financially, but problems began to come to the surface in the bedroom. As Lesley said, "The one thing I needed him to do, he wouldn't do it—I'm sorry, but it was cunnilingus, you know, oral sex. And I am like, you need to figure that out...people do that these days." Ted became upset about this issue, telling Lesley that "he had talked to his girlfriends about it, and they don't like it either. And I'm like, your girlfriends are lying to you."

Lesley further told Ted, "Even if you never get to the point where you want to do this, I think you need to understand why you have a block in certain areas about sex; you need to learn how to relax."

I asked Lesley if Ted wanted her to perform fellatio on him. She responded, "Yeah, all of the time." She noted, "It wasn't just about the act. It was about the giving and reciprocal nature of it. It bothered me that he could hold off on something I wanted. Made me wonder what else in our physical world are you holding back on? And so it got to the point that I started holding back on things he liked because he was holding back on me. That felt so weird to me."

I asked Lesley if she felt that Ted denying her oral sex while wanting her to perform fellatio felt demeaning in any way. Did it make her think about the historical sexual relationship between white men and black women, where black women were subservient to a slave owner's sexual proclivities?

Lesley responded, "Yeah, exactly. I felt that I was falling on my knees on a regular basis with no reciprocation. And that was creating a really unequal relationship I didn't want to have."

Lesley continued by noting, "I saw pictures of some of the white girls that Ted went to college formals with, and they were kind of mousey, plain girls. He hadn't become the handsome guy he is today. And so I know those girls probably did whatever he wanted them to do; they were just thankful he paid them any attention." Moreover Lesley told Ted, "I had a career before I met you. I've been around different places and exposed myself to things I hadn't been able to do as a child...so you need to step up. I'm not like those girls who you once knew."

Over time, the sexual issue between them began to loom larger in their relationship. Lesley remembers feeling that "well, you are supposed to be married until you die. So I thought, well, I would not talk about this for long periods or deal with it. I kind of felt like, eventually, we're going to figure this out together because we love each other, and that's what you do when you are committed to each other."

Ted responded to the sexual tension in their marriage by changing his behavior. He started coming home late from work drunk. Lesley recalled that she had an alcoholic uncle who her family had to deal with and she was not about to go through this with Ted. She asked Ted how she could help him, realizing that he was going through some pain and essentially 'checking out' from their marriage. Not long afterwards, Ted came home one day from work and told Lesley that he wanted a divorce. He told her that he loved her, but knew he was not 'in love' with her.

Their divorce occurred fairly quickly because they told the judge they had been separated for six months. Lesley notes, "I thought I had a good marriage with the one big thing I needed to work on. I for damn sure am not going to have a really bad divorce that's just going to piss all over everything that we've done. ...like I said, we traveled together, bought a house and a car together."

In retrospect Lesley believes that Ted wanted out of the marriage so quickly because he was beginning to feel overwhelmed and pressured from her. He knew she was ready to have children, and he wasn't. Between the sexual issue in their marriage and her desire to get pregnant, Lesley believes Ted had difficulty being honest with her.

Lesley is sorry she didn't take time to speak to a marriage counselor before she agreed to the divorce. She resents that she had to sell their home to settle the divorce. However, now that she is single again, she recognizes a lot of pressure in the relationship is off her, too.

Postscript on Lesley: Two years after her divorce, Lesley reconnected with a black man she had known when she was in her twenties.

He was engaged to get married, but when he learned that he had a life-threatening illness, his fiancé called off the wedding. Lesley took care of this man until his death two years later. Ted remarried within two years of their divorce.

CANDACE

Candace is thirty-seven years old and recently divorced after six years of marriage to Pat. They are both employed as television news anchors and enjoyed a high profile society lifestyle. I met Candace through her aunt. Petite, outgoing and attractive, Candace became subdued when asked about her divorce. She started our conversation by noting that Pat and she had met through a networking event for media professionals in New York. When they discovered that they were both searching for positions in television, they agreed to 'coach' each other and stay in touch. Candace noted that Pat was very attractive, had an easy going manner and projected a confident air. She was attracted to his confidence, wishing she felt as self-assured as he did. She believes Pat was attracted to her because he was the type to enjoy being 'in charge' and probably appreciated her unabashed admiration.

Initially their relationship was long distance. Pat lived in New York and Candace was able to get a local anchor position in a small southern city. Missing the excitement of New York, Candace would arrange to return every few weeks. She stayed with a girlfriend when in New York, but also made time to see Pat. She thinks he was flattered by her attention and eventually their relationship became romantic.

I asked Candace if she had any reservations about dating Pat. After all, their relationship was long distance, and he was in a city where he would have plenty of other women to choose from, especially being in a relatively high profile position. Candace responded, "Yes, I did think of those two things as well as his race, but where I was living then the pickings were pretty slim. I may as well take my chances with him."

Candace continued by noting that Pat did have other girlfriends, and she knew most likely they were white or Latina, but that didn't bother her because Pat seemed pretty oblivious to the race issue. "I never felt he would choose a white woman or Latina woman over me because I am black. I never got that kind of vibe. Even now [after their divorce], I still think the same way."

Candace and Pat dated for two and a half years before getting married. She admitted to being anxious to get married and move away from the city where she was living. Candace remembers the first three years of their marriage going along pretty smoothly. "We had the usual kind of adjustment arguments, but nothing serious. I have other friends whose marriages seemed to bring on more serious arguments." She also notes that neither of their families gave them any problems either. "Basically, we were from similar backgrounds, family-wise, liberal kind of people all around."

With seemingly few problems, I asked Candace what brought on the divorce. She responded, "My career took off far faster than his. I got a couple of lucky breaks. It was hard for him to see my star continue to rise while his didn't. Remember, our relationship from the beginning was based on his being the one 'in charge' and me trying to learn from him. When these roles seemed to be reversing, he wasn't comfortable with this."

Moreover, despite discussing the topic of children before getting married, once Candace's career began to escalate, she wasn't interested in losing momentum by taking off from work to start a family. She concedes that Pat felt betrayed; he was forty years old and felt he would rather have children while he was younger and had the energy to enjoy them. Candace noted that in the news anchor business, an older man is far more common than an older woman. Not thinking that her career would outshine Pat's, she envisioned him being the 'star' while she had a lesser role, in which case, having children would have been easier. "Now that the situation was reversed, I knew I wasn't established enough to walk away and expect to come back at the level I had been. Who knew if I would get these kind of opportunities again?"

The tension in their marriage continued to escalate until one morning while they were having breakfast, she looked at Pat and said, "Don't you think we have put each other through enough? Why become enemies now? We can both walk away and try to remain friends." Candace said she had unknowingly chosen the right moment to have this conversation with him, and she "watched him take this all in. After a few minutes, he looked at me and agreed I was right…end things before they got worse. I think we also realized that right then, all we were splitting up was material stuff; sure, there was going to be some emotional pain, but at least no children were involved. It took a while for us to actually file for divorce, but when we did, surprisingly, it wasn't as bad as it could have been."

Postscript on Candace: She is still working as a news anchor, living independently, and not dating anyone as of this writing. Her ex-husband recently began dating a Latina woman.

DIANE

Diane is thirty-two years old and was married for four years. As a baby she was adopted by a white family and grew up in a small, blue-collar, working class Illinois town where she met her husband in high school. The high school was integrated and she recalls that most of the students either went to community college, the Armed Services, or a training program after graduation. It was not unusual for the students to 'hook up' after high school either by getting married or just living together. In recalling her high school years, Diane stated that her boyfriend and she began dating exclusively when they were juniors. Their families knew each other, even if they weren't particularly friendly, but at the same time none of their parents objected to their relationship, most likely because they didn't realize how close her boyfriend and she had become. She noted that her boyfriend and she became sexually active by the time they were seniors and she was pregnant with their son when they graduated.

Diane and Tim didn't tell any of their parents that she was pregnant until it became obvious that she was gaining weight. They had considered abortion but because they were still 'in love' they didn't want to end the pregnancy. When they told their parents about the pregnancy, her parents were upset and disappointed and Tim's parents told him that he needed to get a better job. Diane's parents eventually became more supportive and agreed to allow her to continue living at home while she went through her pregnancy, with the caveat that she remain in school (she had enrolled in a community college), and Tim pay child support.

Approximately a year after their son was born, Diane and Tim married. While they had planned to get married, Diane noted that her parents especially encouraged them to do so because they didn't want the stigma of her having a bi-racial baby without a husband. "People all know each other's business where I live; my parents didn't want me or themselves to be the source of gossip." Also, Diane admitted that there were probably some folks who would look down on her for having a baby by a white guy who didn't marry her.

Diane and Tim got married in a civil ceremony when they were twenty years old, with a backyard reception for their families and friends. Diane remembers that day as being one of the happiest days of her life. After the celebration, Diane and Tim went back to their apartment (by this time they were living together) and resumed their regular lives.

Diane's mother became the primary caregiver for her grandson. While Diane believes Tim's parents loved their grandson, they weren't able to help much with childcare because of their work schedules.

Once Diane graduated from the community college, she became interested in continuing on to a four-year nursing degree program. Around the same time, Tim became interested in joining the Navy. It was while Tim was away from home and Diane was in nursing school that she met Bruce. Bruce was African American, twelve years older than Diane, and very attracted to her. Diane recalls recognizing that Bruce's age was also a sign of his maturity. He was definitely at that point in his life where he was ready to settle down, and she began questioning her earlier choices to have a baby and get married. Diane said that Bruce's maturity was a real attraction for her even though she still loved Tim. The problem became that Tim was away for long periods of time which left her feeling lonely and vulnerable. She admits to having an 'emotional affair' with Bruce, but realized he was not looking to break up her marriage. Moreover, after two years of being away from home for long periods of time, Tim was eager for them to move to a larger urban environment as soon as Diane finished school. Diane was reluctant to leave their hometown because it would mean several lifestyle adjustments at once. Her parents had provided the support she needed to have a pretty regular life for a young woman with a child and a husband away in the service. This issue became a source of escalating tension in Diane's marriage. She realized Tim had become worldlier than she was and that it was unfair to expect he would be content returning to their small town life. On the other hand, she wasn't interested in starting over in a new city without any social supports, especially when where she was living, there was an employment opportunity awaiting her once she finished her degree. This issue eventually caused Diane and Tim to divorce. As Diane put it, "In the end, we both just wanted different things from life in different places. Diane said their divorce was amicable, one reason being that they had already been separated for long stretches of time with Tim being gone with the Navy. She added that the separation had caused her to view Tim in a different way, "more like a brother than a husband." She admits that there were lots of lonely times after they agreed to divorce but getting through nursing school kept her on track.

Postscript on Diane: As of this writing, she is employed as a nurse and married to Bruce, with whom she has a second son.

LINDA

Linda is forty-five years old and was married to Harold for twenty years. They met when both of them were in medical school on the East Coast. After receiving their medical degrees, they successfully applied for fellowships in Germany. They got married in Germany and over the next decade had two children. When their fellowships ended they moved back to the United States, accepting employment at two Massachusetts hospitals. Linda worked part-time while raising their children and both sets of grandparents visited often, giving Linda and Harold time to vacation by themselves.

Linda believed she had a great life until one day when she had been married for fifteen years, she discovered that Harold was having an affair with one of the young interns at the hospital. When confronted about the affair, Harold told her the truth, acknowledging that he knew he was wrong, but the "thrill of having a young woman romantically interested in him" was too much to resist. Linda was devastated but thought that Harold was simply going through a mid-life crisis. She also acknowledged that between working part-time and being the primary parent, she hadn't paid much attention to Harold's needs. When she saw a photo of the pretty young white woman who had captured Harold's attention, she realized that her marriage was in jeopardy and asked Harold to go with her for marriage counseling. Harold agreed to do so, and his parents offered to keep their grandchildren over the summer to give them time to sort out their lives.

At counseling, Harold admitted to feeling unloved by Linda, that in the years they had been married, her attention had completely shifted from him to their children. He acknowledged that the long hours he worked left him feeling unappreciated and vulnerable. They agreed to try to repair their marriage, primarily because they both wanted to keep their family together. Linda stated that for the next year and a half, both of them tried to keep the marriage together, but it became evident to her that Harold was not happy. She admits to not fully feeling she could trust Harold even though she never caught him being unfaithful again. However, he began to drink more than he once did and, according to Linda, it appeared that he was just 'existing', not really living. He took more time with their children, but even this didn't seem to satisfy him.

They went back to marriage counseling for a few months, where they finally decided that divorce was their best course of action. Two years later their divorce was final. Linda stated that their divorce was not acrimonious; they share custody of their children and both sets of grandparents are still involved in their grandchildren's lives. I asked Linda if she felt race had anything to do with their divorce (after all, Harold had an affair with a young white woman), to which she responded, "Not in any way I can think of. I am sure there are people who would point their finger and say that Harold probably wanted to return to a white woman, but I know this isn't true. You don't stay married for twenty years if you want to be married to someone else. I still think his midlife crisis is to blame, and me not recognizing the signs of burnout. Most people don't realize how many hours doctors work and then when you get home, you don't have that much time to give to your family. It's easy to start thinking the grass may be greener on the other side."

Postscript on Linda: She is dating another white doctor and Harold is dating a colleague, not the intern with whom he had the affair.

PATRICIA

Patricia met her former husband when she was thirty-five years old. He was five years younger. They met at a mutual friend's party on the north side of Chicago. It turned out they lived only two blocks from each other. James initiated the relationship by beginning a conversation with her at the party. According to Patricia, he was very attracted to black culture, including the music, food and black Southern Baptist churches. Patricia said that when James started talking to her she had no idea that he would become someone she dated. However, she "just responded in my usual friendly manner" and found she enjoyed talking with him. Moreover, she admitted that James was very handsome.

Patricia said that James and she became friends as they got to know each other, recognizing they were at similar life stages. They both wanted to settle down and have a family. Patricia recalled that James was so interested in having children that he had even tried to adopt a black child as a single person, but this didn't happen.

They dated a year and a half before they married. No one from either family openly objected to their relationship. Patricia stated that her parents were just glad she was finally getting married. When James introduced her to his mother, she was very gracious and warm;

however, his father was not nearly as accepting. He didn't do anything to try and prevent their marriage, but he often made racially insensitive comments which embarrassed his wife and daughter. Patricia noted that James' father had little impact on their relationship and he died within three to four years after the marriage. James' sister had dated a black man before she married, and this didn't bother his mother either. Patricia believes that his mother's experience with her daughter's boyfriend made it easier for both of them to accept her. James and Patricia married in downtown Chicago at the courthouse with a justice of the peace. Patricia never wanted a big wedding, irrespective of the groom's race. They wanted to start a family right away since they were older than many people marrying for the first time, but this didn't happen. Patricia underwent many painful fertility procedures only to find out that James had a low sperm count, which made conception difficult. When she didn't become pregnant within the first two years of their marriage, they adopted their son.

They were married for 15 years before they divorced. According to Patricia, they got divorced because over time their lives went in separate directions and they hardly spent any time together. For example, James and she attended different churches. He joined a very traditional black Southern Baptist church located on Chicago's south side, where he was a very involved member, and even sang in the choir. Patricia said he was the only white church member, which didn't bother him at all. Patricia went to a majority white church in Evanston, where they lived. She said, "Over time, we just had different interests. He wanted to move closer to his Chicago church and I wasn't interested in doing that. He became very religious; he sincerely loved his Southern Baptist church. However, this faith was not to my liking. Racial issues didn't have anything to do with our divorce with the exception that my husband simply enjoyed being around black people. He didn't see the social issues which surround them." Patricia stated that the only contact she keeps with her former spouse is through their son. They don't talk otherwise. "He never remarried, even though I think he would like to."

Postscript on Patricia: "Currently, I am dating a white man again; just by coincidence, someone I have known more than 50 years from my hometown in western Illinois. We have been going out for two years. I didn't initiate the relationship; he did. I always saw him as more of a platonic friend. He decided he wanted to take the relationship to another level two years ago, even though he has been a bachelor all of his life. It is nice to have a friend like him at this stage in my life. We know each other so well. I usually prefer black men, but since there are so few around, I believe in taking love where you can find it—as long as it is a good relationship. Two people who understand and trust each other."

SUMMARY

The ten narratives featured in this chapter on black women divorced from white husbands indicate typical reasons why many marriages end. Notably, in the majority of cases, race or racial issues were not contributing factors in the divorce.

CHAPTER 7

WHITE MEN ON DATING BLACK WOMEN

To provide balance to my research on interracial relationships between black women and white men, I decided to interview in-depth five of these men individually. Their perspectives on black women are illuminating. Unfortunately, most studies on interracial relationships ignores the viewpoints of white men.

DAVID

David is in his middle 50s and has exclusively dated black women for most of his life. He was married to one black woman for fifteen years, ended a live-in relationship with a second black woman after five years, and is currently in a third relationship with a black woman which he hopes will lead to marriage.

David bears a strong resemblance to the actor Al Pacino.

I began my interview with David by asking him to tell me about himself, his background, and why he prefers black women. He responded by telling me that he had grown up in an urban area, had many black friends growing up, and through his work had gotten to know several black women. He had a long history of involvement with civil rights and other community issues. As a result, he had a comfort level with black people and enjoyed the honest camaraderie.

David met the three black women in his life through work. He observed that black women were more interesting to him. He appreciated the independent attitude most of the women he knew had. He stated, "I never had the impression that black women were waiting on me to take charge in the relationship. They were perfectly comfortable doing what they wanted; they weren't relying on me to make decisions. I felt as if we were partners in the relationship. I wasn't the leader, which I think is healthier in a relationship."

David said that his first marriage ended because of her infidelity (she had a long term affair with her boss), and his second relationship ended because he wasn't ready to marry again and his girlfriend wanted to have children. In his current relationship, he notes that this girlfriend has been married before and is in no hurry to remarry; she just basically wants companionship.

I asked David how his family felt about his preference for black women. He replied that neither of his parents gave him any 'flak' about this and further, he is not the only one in his family to date interracially. He has two female cousins whose spouses are African American and Mexican American, respectively, "so race was not much of an issue in my family." He added that his parents were more concerned about his girlfriends' values, what kinds of families they came from, if they attend church…those sorts of issues. His mother would comment that, she "didn't mind having a United Nations family as long as we were really united."

I asked David why more white men weren't dating black women. He responded, "I don't know. I think that is a complicated question. First of all, sometimes it's hard to know if a black woman is interested in you [white males]. I always had to make the first approach, which is not necessarily the case with white women. Second, I have worked with some black women who basically treated me as if I were one of their brothers, not a potential romantic interest. I was just one of the guys. And that's not necessarily a bad thing because I feel I actually know some of them better than if they were trying to impress me."

I asked David if he had experienced any negative racial incidents while married or dating, to which he replied, "yes." He noted that "in some places, restaurants, bars, you may get more attentive service if you are with other whites. There are white bartenders and wait staff that aren't as friendly when they see you are with someone black. But you know what? I have seen black couples get better service than me with a black woman. Crazy."

I asked David if he felt dating and marriage to a black woman had cost him in any way. He responded, "No, not at all. I work in an integrated environment and have always felt accepted by my coworkers. I know some of my black female colleagues knew my wife was black, which was actually a positive because I think they thought I could relate easier to them. And I don't have any friends who cared that my wife was black. I can't imagine I would be living any differently if I were married to a white woman."

I asked David how he got along with his first wife's and current girlfriend's families. He replied that in the case of his wife, "her mother was pretty warm to me, but it took me a while to get her father to accept me. He wasn't mean or anything…I would just say wary. By the time we had been married for a few years, he realized that I wasn't going to go away and our relationship got closer. When my wife and I divorced and they learned she had had an affair, they were irritated with her and, I think, felt sorry for me. I still call them from time to time; as long as we had been married, I don't think it is right to just drop people…and they know I am not fishing for any information on Jackie" (his former wife).

Finally, I asked David if he had any advice for black women who may be interested in dating interracially. He responded, "Just be yourself…don't think of a white man as any different from any other man you may be interested in…we are just people."

JIM

Jim is in his forties and has been dating his first black girl-friend for three years. When I asked Jim how he came to be dating a black woman, his response was, "I don't think of it as dating a black woman; I just know I'm dating Rhonda." I asked Jim if he had ever had any interest in dating outside of his race prior to Rhonda, to which he replied, "Not really, but then I grew up in a mostly middle class, white bread suburb" [of Chicago]. There weren't many African Americans—or any other minority groups, for that matter—at his high school. It wasn't until he went away to college at a Big Ten university that he met "lots of people from different backgrounds" in his classes and living in his first residence hall. Jim indicated that he enjoyed the stimulation of interacting with new people who held different political views from his own and joined a couple of student groups to "get outside of the mindset I had grown up around." Jim indicated further that he didn't have an exclusive girlfriend in college, but did hang out and party like everyone else he knew on the weekends. He pointed out that most of the bars he went to or the parties he attended were integrated. "Only a few of the fraternities were still all-white and even some of their parties brought in a mix of students." Jim feels that his college experience provided the foundation for him becoming more open-minded about the world in general. "I came to realize that basically everyone wants the same things out of life, but some people have greater advantages than others… not the fault of those who don't have as much."

After college Jim got his first job in advertising, which he enjoyed, but within three years he was looking for employment at a larger firm. He landed his second position at an advertising agency in Chicago, where he met Rhonda. She was his boss. Jim said he didn't have any reservations working for Rhonda, but "to be honest, if she had been white, I would have been a little more wary because in my former position, I found that the women [white] I worked with were mostly concerned about looking professional and climbing the career ladder. I know it is tough for a woman to make it big time in the corporate world, and to do so, some of them had gone overboard [in terms of attitude]. I think they figured I would be their competition so they weren't all that friendly."

"Rhonda was not like the white women I had worked with at all. She was very professional, always dressed well, but still friendly… and not just on the surface." He wound up working on several important projects with Rhonda and as a result got to know her pretty well. He noted, "Even though she was my boss, she never tried to exert her authority. She figured we were both working for the same team and once told me, 'We sink or swim together.'" Jim further observed that Rhonda wasn't bossy with any of the other staff members under her either. "Most people felt she was a great supervisor; knew what she was doing, what you should be doing, and expected you to do it."

Whenever their working hours ran late, Rhonda and Jim would grab dinner before returning to the office. Jim got up the nerve to ask her out, as "I had grown quite comfortable with her. She didn't accept, telling me that she didn't mix business with pleasure, but appreciated I thought of her in that way." Eventually Jim changed jobs, but would still see Rhonda at professional meetings. Following one of these meetings, he asked her if she would consider going out, "just to catch up on what had been happening in our lives since I had left her firm, and she said sure." Rhonda and Jim continued to date, casually at first, and then more seriously. Jim stated that he was attracted to Rhonda because she was different from the other women he had met in his field, she was pretty, and they had a lot in common. "Of course, she has issues to deal with that I don't, and I know some of these include race as well as the fact that she is a woman...but I like the way she manages her career and still is a nice person. She isn't threatened by me in any way and in fact, once commented that she was glad we had each other's back." Jim further admitted that he thought Rhonda was "very sexy in a good way...but she doesn't act like she knows it."

I asked Jim if he found dating a black woman different from dating a white woman, to which he responded, "I don't think I have enough dating experience to answer that question, but I can tell you that if Rhonda is typical of other black women, then I would say they [black women] have a softer side, maybe a more egalitarian attitude toward relationships. They don't seem to be caught up in all of the b.s. most of the white women I know are. Rhonda keeps it real."

Postscript on Jim and Rhonda: They are engaged and plan to marry next year.

PATRICK

Patrick is thirty years old and grew up on Chicago's south side in an Irish Catholic family and neighborhood. Patrick went to Catholic schools, including a high school where there were few African American or other minority students. He noted that the Catholic league sports teams tended to be fairly segregated and when his school had to play games at an all-black high school, there was plenty of discussion around the dinner table prior to the game. Patrick indicated that his natural personality tends to be fairly open and curious, and he was disturbed when he read various interpretations of American history and saw how blacks and other minorities were portrayed. He observed that his parents had grown up in Chicago as well and lived in neighborhoods from which his grandparents fled when African Americans started moving in. He believes that his parents and their friends hold some prejudice against blacks because they resented having to move from their neighborhoods as a part of 'white flight.' In their minds, they felt blacks took over their neighborhoods, so they never quite got along with them. Patrick said he grew up with his parents' prejudices and didn't try to get to know the black students. He also stated that when he went to games, he was never attracted to any of the black cheerleaders.

When it came time for him to go to college, Patrick wanted to spread his wings a bit, since he came to realize that he was living in a pretty homogenous, closed community. He went to Vanderbilt University, where he was exposed to people from around the world.

During his first semester, he met a black girl who was from San Diego to whom he was attracted. He remembers thinking he wanted to get to know her better and that he could not "not date her because of anything his family or her family would say." In his mind, "this would have been wrong and go against my values." So they started dating right from the beginning of his freshman year.

One day when he was home for Christmas break, his father and he were sitting in their den watching The O'Reilly Show' and Bill O'Reilly was discussing immigration issues. During a commercial break, his father asked him how his first semester had gone in a casual sort of way. Patrick said he told him about a few of his college experiences when his father then asked, "Well, are you dating anyone? Got a girlfriend?" Patrick said his stomach dropped and he thought, *Uh-oh...here it comes.* He responded, "Yeah, I do" and his father then asked, "So what's her name?" Patrick replied, "Christina." His father then said, "Christina...so is she Greek?" To which Patrick replied, "No" and his father said, "Well then, what's her last name?" Patrick replied, "Grady." His father said, "Oh, so she's Irish?" And Patrick said, "No...getting colder." "So he was like...so what is she?" Patrick then plunged in with, "Well, she's actually black, African American." Patrick said his father did not respond for what seemed a long, pregnant pause, and then said, "Well, you know, it's 2005 and times have changed...we've come a long way." Patrick was surprised by his father's words, and breathed a sigh of relief, then said to his father, "Honestly, I thought you were going to take this [his news] harder than this." To which his father responded, "Come on, you aren't dating a black girl, are you?" To which Patrick replied, "Yes, I really am and she is darker skinned." After what Patrick described as another long pause his father looked at him and asked, "So have you told your mother?" Patrick replied that he hadn't yet, and his father then said, "Why don't you go tell your mother?"

In reflecting on this exchange Patrick said that he realized his father "needed a minute to take this news in. He wasn't prepared to hear that I had a black girlfriend."

Patrick then went into the kitchen to tell his mother and her response was similar to his father's.

I asked Patrick why he thought his parents were interested in his girlfriend's ethnicity; was it common for his parents to want to know this information so early in a relationship? Patrick replied, "It wasn't unusual for my parents to ask this question because they are pretty 'old school.' It is something they would want to know. I was just caught off guard by how soon this conversation came up when I got home. In the neighborhood that I grew up in, people were segregated not only by race, but also by ethnicity." His neighborhood was largely Irish Catholic; not far from his neighborhood is Midway airport where the surrounding community is largely Polish. Patrick said his parents would not have objected if he were dating a Polish girl, "but they were probably counting on me dating an Irish Catholic girl."

I asked Patrick to tell me how of all of the girls at Vanderbilt, he was attracted to Christina. Patrick responded, "Of all of the girls around campus, Christina was very special, very out-going, probably the most extroverted girl I have ever met. She was the life of the party, the most fun…vibrant, attractive…really different from all of the other girls I have known. She was from California, and I had made up my mind that when I went to college I wanted to meet people from other places...she was very interesting to me. Sure, I could have dated a white woman, but I knew a lot of white women from home."

I asked Patrick how Christina and he actually started dating. He replied that one day he ran into Christina in their dorm hallway and he just asked her if she wanted to go out for dinner. She agreed and he remembers that their first date was at Chili's restaurant. From that first date, their relationship just continued to grow. "We would study in the lounge in our dorm, and then take breaks to get something to eat."

I asked Patrick if they had experienced any trouble while out in public. He responded, "One of the things that surprised me was Nashville, and the student body, and the South in general didn't seem as racist as my neighborhood. It [racism] was definitely still there, but I never heard the 'n' word openly, nor did anyone say anything racist to us. One thing I remember is that Christina got a lot of dirty looks directed at her from other black women. Back home though, there was probably a different story."

After his parents digested his news, Patrick felt they exerted subtle pressure to break up his relationship. For the rest of his visit, "my father was kind of silent about my news. My mom asked me, 'Are you sure you want to do this? This is really hard. If you married this girl, your kids may have trouble.'" I replied, "None of that is important to me, I am not going to kowtow to society pressures. I think they were most concerned about what the rest of the family and their friends would say when they found out about my relationship. My parents were like, 'we don't want to be in this fight [fighting racial tension].' By virtue of me dating Christina, they felt forced into this situation." [dealing with racism]

I asked Patrick how his two older sisters responded to his dating a black woman. He replied that "at first one of my sisters was put off by it....but of course, this is the sister whose last boyfriend was black." Patrick's other sister, who he described as being 'more like my mom' told him that "she didn't think it was a good idea [his interracial relationship]. She is the type of person to be concerned about the logistics of things, such as where was I going to live if I married a black woman...most likely I wouldn't be able to live around them [his family], what about if you have kids, how do you think they will feel? She said to me, 'You know, relationships are hard enough to maintain as it is; why would you want to add this additional layer to yours?'"

When I asked Patrick how Christina's family felt about their relationship, he replied, "Christina is from California, her parents are both lawyers and they are pretty well off. They were used to living around and socializing with whites. Her having a white boyfriend was no big thing for them. She didn't catch any flack about me." Patrick noted that most of his interactions were with Christina's mother, "who always treated me great." He didn't have as many interactions with her father because the parents were divorced and Christina lived primarily with her mother.

Patrick admitted to feeling a little awkward sometimes around some of his white male college friends, especially if they started using the 'n' word. However, when he would give them a look "like really?" some were quick to point out that they weren't referring to Christina.

When he brought Christina home to meet his parents for a weekend and took her to a couple of local bars he used to frequent, he did get looks from some of the other patrons. One time at a bar, the bartender quickly switched off the music and put on something entirely different. A longtime friend of his said, "You know, Patrick, there are 'n's and there are black people. We just don't want no 'n's around here."

I asked Patrick how Christina's first visit home went for them. He visited her family in San Diego the summer following their freshman year. Christina visited his family over the Christmas break. Christina stayed at his home; his parents had met her earlier at a college football game and treated her well. Patrick noted that despite his parent's prejudices, they aren't hateful people, and welcomed her like any other guest.

Patrick learned from his mother that his relationship had caused a strain on his parents' marriage. His mother was annoyed with his father that he hadn't told his grandmother [Patrick's father's mother] about Patrick's relationship. Patrick feels the reason for this was that his father "didn't want to hear any shit from his brothers [Patrick's uncles]." According to Patrick, it was so ironic that his father didn't tell his grandmother about his relationship because she was undoubtedly the most liberal person in the family. He noted that his grandmother was very involved in trying to make Chicago Lawn [a previously all-white, racially segregated Chicago south side neighborhood] a more racially tolerant and welcoming community when blacks started to move in. She worked with a Catholic priest who wrote a book about his experience trying to desegregate this neighborhood where he specifically mentioned his grandmother's contributions. However, Patrick stated that his father has one brother "who is an asshole, and very prejudiced." Most likely his father didn't want to have to hear any comments about Patrick's relationship from him. Patrick admitted to getting into a very heated argument with this uncle over his relationship and vowing to keep him out of his life in the future.

I asked Patrick what his family thought about Christina after their first five-day visit. Patrick said his mother thought Christina was too bossy, that she corrected him too much. Christina would say things to him such as, "Sit up straight." Patrick agreed with his mother that Christina was too bossy and argumentative, but thinks her behavior was just a component of being extroverted.

Patrick indicated that Christina and he dated for several years, at times off and on. According to Patrick, they were each other's first sexual relationship and their sex life was always good. "Great in fact…kept us together through a lot of other stuff."

So what caused them to break up? According to Patrick, "we both wanted to steer the ship…and with her being the daughter of two lawyers, I got tired of always arguing." The break-up was pretty hard on both of them; "we should have broken up probably two years before we did, but it was really hard to let go. We wound up dating long distance a few times, which eventually made it easier to break up for good."

Postscript on Christina: She is engaged to another white guy, living in the D.C. area, and working as a project manager.

Patrick continued to date black women and met his second black girlfriend, an African from Ghana, online while in graduate school in the D.C. area. He also started to analyze why he is attracted to black women. According to Patrick, despite all of the complicated psycho-analyses he thinks it comes down to the fact that once you have a serious relationship with a woman that lasts for a long time, you are naturally attracted to other women you think are the same type.

However, with his Ghanian girlfriend he also learned the importance of culture. He learned that many Africans look down on African Americans, which was the case with his Ghanian girlfriend and her family, something he would never have considered. He introduced his Ghanian girlfriend [Nana] to his parents, and he knows they liked her better than Christina. There wasn't as much of a learning curve for his parents, and Nana was more traditional in her views than Christina. His relationship with Nana lasted for two years. When she left to go to graduate school in Germany, their relationship fizzled out.

Patrick is currently in a relationship with his third black girlfriend, who he thinks he is going to marry. They have been dating for nearly two years and living together for about a year. "She is from Michigan and grew up in a middle class African American family. She understands racial issues better than Christina. She is also of mixed race, some Italian ancestry." They get along well, have fun, and have similar family backgrounds. She is a nurse midwife. They met online. She liked the fact that he "didn't need any training… really understands African American culture. She told me that she was open to dating white men as long as she didn't have to teach them about black culture. She likes that I get it. She liked the fact that I had taught in the inner city, and knew what to say and not to say." Also, "she was impressed I understood all the hair type issues and stuff like that." Patrick said his parents like his current girlfriend a lot; they are 'so over it' [the race component]. He noted that they are at a time in their lives when they don't care what other people think anymore. "They have adjusted to the fact that I prefer black women, and they are like whatever. My sister started dating a black guy a couple of years after I was dating Christina, something I take partial credit for." Patrick laughed when he said he knows his parents have been teased because his sister and he have dated black people. "There must be something in the water in the Byrne house."

I asked Patrick if he had encountered any problems living in the Logan Square neighborhood with a black girlfriend. Patrick said there have been a few black men who have hollered out comments from car windows at his girlfriend, asking, "Why you dating that white boy? " Patrick noted that the same thing happened when he was dating Nana in Washington, D.C. The white people in Logan Square are mostly hippie types, no one seems to be paying them much attention.

In concluding our interview, I asked Patrick to finish the following sentence: 'I am attracted to black women because…' and he replied, "I like curves, and black women generally are far curvier than white women. I am not into skinny women. I don't find thin white women very attractive."

Postscript on Patrick: He is engaged to his girlfriend and they plan to marry later this year.

MATTHEW

Matthew is in his late 40s and grew up on Chicago's far south side, eventually moving to a south suburban community. His neighborhood was integrated and he attended high school with whites, blacks and Hispanics. After he graduated from high school, he joined the Marines, spending four years in the service. He got married for the first time after leaving the Marines, had three children, and several years later divorced. He married a second time and this marriage also ended in divorce. Both of his wives were white; his current girlfriend, Evette, is black.

However, she is not the first black woman he has dated. He dated two black women when he was nineteen and living on the Marine base. Both of the women worked there.

Matthew indicated that over time and through all of his dating experiences, he has come to understand that he gets along better with black women. "They [black women] get me in a way that neither of my wives did. I look at myself, and I think that I'm a little different...which can cause problems in all of my relationships, but Evette doesn't get on me about stuff the way my wives did. My current girlfriend is an easier connection; I don't faze her. She has a good sense of humor...I can be myself. I find that I am more comfortable around blacks of both sexes. My experience of black people is that they are far more accepting of others, far more than whites. I have had people from both races ask me why I hang around with black people so much. I have to tell them…they accept me for who I am, I don't have to be anyone other than myself with them."

Growing up Matthew said he knew several black people. He was aware of the neighborhood boundaries and people tended to stay with just their own kind. He said that being in the service forced him to live outside of the racial bubbles. Prior to joining the service, he felt limited as to where he could go in Chicago. The racism of the time imposed boundaries on blacks and whites. He feels that the service breaks down many racial boundaries; it may be the first time for both groups that they get to know each other.

After his second divorce, he decided to go back to school. "Life is about growth. I learned so much about myself going to school. I made amends with my former wives; we are pretty much friends now. I learned the most about myself from my relationships with black women. They forced me not only to learn about life, but about myself."

Matthew said he would have been dating black girls in high school but he was afraid. "I was too shy to talk to any of the girls, black or white, back then, but I remember this one black girl who I had a crush on. She was so pretty, but the guys gave me a hard time, saying, 'You think she would seriously be interested in you?'"

Matthew said he didn't get any objections to dating black women from his family. If any of his family members didn't like it, they never said anything to him. He ran into trouble when dating black women when he was living in the South. He observed that while he was on base that there were no problems, but if he ventured into the town, "I got a lot of looks from people, black and white."

Matthew further explained that most of the black women he dated were darker skinned, and this meant they always stood out as a couple. "I didn't think much about it, but for sure people thought of us as an interracial couple...and I could tell that this ruffled a few feathers."

Despite his experience in the South, Matthew noted that one of the most racist incidences he had was a few summers ago in Chicago on the north side. He was invited to a party by some white people that he knows who live in the Wrigleyville area. While they aren't close friends, he decided to go with Evette because it was at one of the harbors. He said that when they walked into the party "you would have thought we had three heads by the looks we got from the other people at the party." Prior to entering the party, when he was trying to figure out how to get into the harbor gate to park his car, the white attendant didn't make any attempt to help him, just made a few odd gestures. When he finally figured out how to get the gate to open, the attendant walked up to the car and, looking at Evette, said, 'Well, I see you finally got in." Matthew said the attendant was somewhat drunk but the way he directed this comment to his girlfriend left no doubt in his mind about the racial implication of his statement.

Matthew said he gets looks and side comments from whites all of the time. Coming out of Wrigley Field one time after a game, there was a group of twenty-something black girls. "Four white guys in a car hollered out the window at them, 'Hey, you go, girls.' Little comments with racist undertones."

Matthew noted that he encountered racist people in both the North and South. He has been called 'nigger lover' and has been asked by other white guys what is wrong with white women. One of his friends who enjoys Barry White's [a black singer] music has nick-named him 'Barely White' due to his preference for black women.

Matthew has also experienced prejudice from black men. One time when he was at a downtown Chicago bar with Evette and another black couple, the guy pulled him to the side and said for him to "be careful…those dudes [other black males at the bar] hate you; they don't like seeing no white boy with a good looking black woman." Matthew responded, "I get that…but if I were black, I would just be another black dude in a bar…so I don't get all worked up. I am prepared for this type of reaction."

Matthew estimated that he has dated seven black women for periods of longer than six months at a time. Evette is his longest rela-tionship, they live together, and they are thinking of getting married. She has been married before, too, and has children and grandchil-dren. They are thinking that once their children are grown (all of the children are teenagers through 20s) and out of the house that they may marry. Matthew said Evette has been very good for him "…always a positive attitude." She teaches second grade and is three years older than him.

I asked Matthew how their children feel about their relation-ship. He responded that his own children have a somewhat frac-tured relationship with him due to the divorce, but he is doing his best to repair it. They have never voiced any negative comments to him about Evette. Matthew has not met Evette's two adult children because they live out of state. He has, however, spoken with them many times by phone. According to Matthew, they are totally fine with their relationship.

I questioned Matthew on how he met Evette. He replied that he was with a friend and they had stopped at a convenience store. He noticed Evette right away, but didn't approach her. She was with one of her girlfriends. After Matthew paid for his items he walked out of the store and waited by the side of his friend's car for him to finish paying for his purchases. While he was standing there, Evette walked out of the store by herself and approached him. She was waiting for her girlfriend to leave the store. Evette spoke to him and the two of them began conversing, just making small talk. After a few minutes, when her girlfriend came out of the store, Evette asked him for his last name and his phone number. He asked her, "if she was going to run a security check on me, to which she smiled and responded, 'Maybe…but I will probably call you sooner than you think.'" He was surprised she did this, but happily complied.

Matthew said he appreciated that Evette was bold and confident enough to make the first move. He thinks more men would appreciate having a woman make the first overture if they are interested. Evette called him two days later and they arranged to go out the following evening. They took a long walk where they talked and then stopped in a restaurant for dinner. The first date lasted about four hours, and they got together again a few nights later.

I asked Matthew if he was the first white man Evette dated. He replied, "No, in fact, I am the third white guy she has dated. She had a serious relationship with one of them, but it didn't last." Evette told him that while her former white boyfriend was a nice person, generous, and treated her well, over time as the relationship became more serious, he became very controlling. He started trying to monitor her behavior, asking her where she was going and who she was with. Evette was not used to being controlled so that element ended their relationship. Matthew was quick to add that he is not controlling, which he knows goes a long way in making their relationship a good one.

I asked Matthew what he would say to other white men who are thinking of dating outside their race. He responded, "If you are interested, just do it...and don't pay attention to any of the stuff that the media puts out about black people and black women. I don't see or read too much positive stuff out there. I think the media and the culture hypersexualize black women. Don't get caught up in that kind of hype. Also, on the first date, don't take her to a soul food restaurant. That is way too patronizing and more than likely if you do this, you won't have a second date."

CHASE

Chase is thirty-nine years old and grew up in a conservative western Chicago suburb. He began our interview by noting that in the town in which he grew up, the only minorities he knew were Asians. His family is very close-knit, a factor which he appreciated, but at times found stifling. After high school he decided to spread his wings, enrolling at a large university in Iowa.

While in college, he interacted with a very diverse group of people, majored in economics, and for the first time made friends with people who weren't white. Upon graduation he moved into Chicago and pursued an MBA while working full-time at a bank.

He met his wife of three years, Vera, at a Chicago club. He was initially a little hesitant about asking her out, but realized that it wasn't because he wasn't attracted her; he just had a few qualms about what his family would think. Chase said that between going to college and living in the city, he had grown accustomed to a broader racial mix, which he found energizing. He thought women of color more interesting than most of the white women he knew, not that he wasn't attracted to white women, but he found dating black or Hispanic women more 'real.' "I didn't feel I had to meet any precon- ceived expectations in the relationships; I felt more relaxed."

Chase observed that by living away from his family, he recog- nized how insulated their lives were.

He described feeling restless, a need to break away from the 'white bread' mold of his youth. "I feel I have gotten to experience so much more [than other family members] because I took a chance and expanded my social network." His wife is the first African American woman he dated, but he also dated two Hispanic women. He said that he had more in common with Vera since she came from a similar social class background and is comparably educated. She is employed in banking, too.

I asked Chase what his family had to say when they learned about Vera. He responded that initially they pretended to be okay with his relationship, but were really worried about what their friends would think. "I think they thought that if they didn't say anything that the relationship would end on its own. They felt that perhaps I was going through a phase after living in the city for a while." Chase thought their perception was funny because "they didn't realize just how much racism is still to be found in Chicago."

He didn't introduce Vera to his family until he knew the relationship was serious. He described their first meeting as friendly, but not as warm as it would have been had Vera been a white woman. Chase acknowledged that his parents and other family members are prejudiced, but also, they are somewhat clannish, and they aren't initially trusting of outsiders. He didn't try to force his relationship on them, but rather allowed his family to 'come around' at their own pace. He believed this was the best strategy he could have taken with them because when they realized his relationship was serious, their attitudes began to soften. His parents didn't want to be the cause of any breach in their relationship with him. He and Vera dated for three and a half years before they married in a small ceremony at the church they both attend. Their immediate family members attended the ceremony and dinner reception afterwards. Chase stated that everyone made the effort to be supportive to ensure that the day went well. Since their marriage, they are both comfortable when visiting each other's families, and he knows his mother is looking forward to the day when Vera and he have children. "She loves being a grandmother."

I asked Chase what specific attributes about Vera attracted him to her. He responded, "We met in probably the most casual way possible; she simply started talking to me while we were waiting for our drink orders to be filled at the bar. She was attractive, an easy person to talk to, intelligent and with no pretense; I could tell immediately she would be fun to be around, and that is still true. She is also pretty independent and slightly irreverent."

Chase indicated further that Vera was completely nonplussed about his family's initial reaction to learning about her. "Her attitude was like, 'What did you expect? Your folks aren't exposed; they probably think most African Americans are thugs from what they see on the news—they haven't been around black people who live just as well as they do." On the other hand, Vera's parents weren't surprised that Chase was white. They live in an integrated community where interracial couples can feel comfortable and have a diverse group of friends. Chase noted that his race didn't seem to be an issue for them, even though they knew how his family initially felt about Vera. I asked Chase what he would tell other white men interested in dating African American women. He quickly responded, "It's not the race or the skin color, it's the woman...the total person. Don't let outside forces prevent you from exploring all of your options for having a fulfilling life."

SUMMARY

The narratives from the five white men interviewed for this chapter give balance to the stories presented by the black women. Most noteworthy is the sensitivity and awareness these white men had about race and racial issues which confront African Americans whether they are in interracial relationships or not.

CHAPTER 8

FREQUENTLY ASKED QUESTIONS AND COMMENTS

When I set out to learn about the experiences of black women who are dating, married to, or divorced from white men, my goal was to present a picture of what it looks like to be in an interracial relationship. Over the past five years, I have spoken with numerous groups and individuals about my research and discovered that the relative uniqueness of my topic evoked interesting questions and comments. I am including a list of the most frequently asked questions as well as my responses in this chapter.

1. Why did you specifically choose black women in relationships with white men as opposed to other non-white men?

American history denotes the numerous ways in which black women were demeaned and disrespected by white men. Black women were never accorded the respect or status of white women, an assessment which is still prevalent. Despite this historical backdrop, the number of interracial marriages between black women and white men is growing. As a sociologist, it was interesting for me to discover how and why relationships between the group highest in the social hierarchy, (white men) and the group lowest in the social hierarchy (black women) occurred.

I purposely did not study black women in relationships with other minority men (i.e., Hispanics (Latinos), Asians, or Africans) because these relationships do not contain equivalent social psychological and historical challenges. The racial dynamics are different even if there may be some initial social and cultural resistance to the relationship from the couples' families. However, it is worth noting that black women are even *less* likely to be married to Asian men than to whites. Asian men generally are *least* likely to marry outside of their cultures, while Asian women are the minority group *most* likely to be married to white men.

2. Were interracial marriages illegal in this country prior to 1967?

The answer to this question is: that depended on the state. Generally, interracial marriages were illegal in many states, primarily in the South, prior to 1967. However, in Northern and Western states public sentiment reduced the likelihood of interracial marriages to the degree that formal laws were not considered necessary.

It is important to note the following:

a) The first Africans who came to America were not enslaved and history denotes they intermarried with other white immigrants and Native Americans (Roberts, 1994).

b) During Reconstruction (1865-1874) historical records suggest a greater latitude in forming interracial marriages, with the result that hundreds of Southern white men married black women (Roberts, 1994).

Research of records from this time period indicate that as laws prohibiting interracial marriages were declared null or void, hundreds, if not thousands, of these marriages took place. Many of these couples had been living together prior to this time period. It is interesting to note that most of the white husbands were foreign born who married their black mistresses or concubines (Roberts, 1994).

3. How have black-white interracial marriages changed in recent times?

Couples embarking on an interracial relationship or marriage today face far fewer social challenges than their older counterparts. I can report that many of the racial tensions and issues older interracial couples experienced are not relevant to younger couples. These couples had experienced significantly fewer racist incidents, less family disapproval, and a greater sense of feeling accepted in society than earlier generations. The growing number of African Americans who are middle class, college educated, and professional accounts in part for the reduction in harsh racial attitudes. Another factor is that Americans overall report greater acceptance of black-white interracial marriage (July 25, 2013 Gallop poll). Finally, a third factor which I believe supports greater acceptance of interracial marriage is what I term 'the browning of America', first by people of color from Mexico and other parts of the world, and second by the growing percentage of the population that identifies as biracial or mixed. Urban demographer and professor, Joel Kotkin wrote in 2010 in his book, *The Next Hundred Million: America in 2050* that the majority of the U.S. population will be comprised of non-white people by then (Kotkin,

2010). He believes "race will always be a marker" in how Americans describe themselves but that it won't be as salient as it has been.

4. Did I perceive any racial fetishism among the couples I interviewed?

Yes—in the case of one couple, it became apparent to me when interviewing them that they were satisfying each other's racial fetish. In the case of the white husband, I detected a sexual fetish with having a curvaceous black wife. As for the black wife, I discerned that her husband met her fantasy of what a white Prince Charming should look like.

Fetishes apparently don't make for lasting relationships, as the couple divorced after five years of marriage. In a follow-up conversation with the wife, she stated, "[ ] was not who I thought he was; I guess he will be on the prowl for his next black Venus...or Adonis." She suggested that her former husband's sexual fetish was most likely due to a latent homosexual orientation. He thought that by marrying her, he would be cured.

5. Age as a factor in interracial relationships

Age tends to play a role in the formation of interracial marriages. Research has suggested that interracial couples are older than their same race counterparts at the time of marriage. (Romano, 2003; Schwartz and Scott, 2000) While this trend continued in my current research, it was not as evident as it was during my first study. However, many of the couples dated or lived together for several years prior to marriage which also meant they were older than couples marrying for the first time. The couples' ages may play a role.

as well in marriage stability and duration. Social science research suggests that the marital pairing of black wives and white husbands tends to be more stable due to the egalitarian nature of many of these marriages.

6. Family Acceptance of the Marriage

One factor which increases family acceptance of an interracial marriage is the birth of grandchildren. When I asked respondents how their relationship with in-laws changed over the course of their marriages, nearly all of them mentioned having children as strengthening family bonds. As one woman observed, "Even if my in-laws didn't initially welcome me into the family, when I had my son, I felt a greater sense of acceptance because now I was the mother of their grandchild, and they didn't want to mess up this relationship."

Moreover, my research indicated that black families are usually more initially accepting than white families of an interracial relationship. However, initial resistance to interracial relationships did come from both groups.

I also think it is important to acknowledge some of the comments I received from blacks and whites when speaking about my research.

Comments from black women included: "So are you sure you want to tackle this issue?" "You are pretty brave to put this problem out in the open." "It is embarrassing that black women don't have the dating opportunities other women have…but what can we do about it?" "No matter what you say, black men are going to resent you telling black women to look outside of the race for husbands, even if they don't marry any of us." "It's great that you are trying to change the mindset of black women, but I think most of us still wish for a black man." "I think your topic is bold and interesting. It will also do a lot of good for frustrated black women. Should open many eyes."

A few black women remained unconvinced that white men would sincerely be interested in dating them. For example, several of the women told me that while they were open to dating outside their race, they didn't pick up any social cues from the white men they knew indicating there was any attraction to them. My response was that there are going to be men from all races who won't be romantically interested in them and for those white men who may be, my research indicated that fear plays a role in why they don't pursue black women.

Another woman asked if I had any suggestions on how to convey interest to a white man.

My answer was to ask how she conveyed interest to a black man. What did she do? Is there a reason why what may work for a man who shares one's race does not work for any other man? As one black man reminded me, "Women do the choosing, whether it be a white woman choosing a black man or a black woman choosing to explore a relationship with a white man. In most cases it will fall to the woman to let a man know she is interested in him, irrespective of race."

Several of the black women interviewed for this book made the first move to convey interest and didn't feel embarrassed if the initial attraction was not reciprocated. They simply moved on to someone else, or met other prospects through friends.

It is also important to note that black women who grew up in integrated communities where they were socialized at an early age with whites found it far easier to initiate a conversation with a white male. These women didn't have the same trepidation in crossing racial boundaries in seeking romantic partners. As one black woman who had spent her childhood in a predominantly white community told me, "Really, a man is a man." Her view, however, is not representative of black women who don't have the same comfort level with whites.

Comments from black men included: "You go ahead and put it out there...black women should feel free to date and marry anybody they want." "I see what you are trying to do, even if it could make us [black men] look bad." "I don't like the idea of black women dating white men, but I do understand why this happens."

Comments from white women: These were most interesting and often began with an awkward silence. However, what emerged from this silence was an underlying respect that I was willing to challenge the status quo—perhaps a tacit acknowledgment that black women didn't have it as easy finding suitable partners as they did. Another frequent response was a sense of guilt, perhaps wondering how or if they were complicit in the dating challenges faced by black women. For most, I brought up a subject they had never considered before, but they were immediately sensitive to what I was saying. A couple of white women remarked that the one thing they had heard was how angry black women were that black men chose white women to marry over them. One young white woman told me that she had taken a college course on marriage and the family, and her white professor made a point of stating "the one thing that will make a black woman angry is seeing a black man with a white woman." This was also the response I received from some black men married to white women when I was interviewing them. One black husband stated, "I don't care how well I know a black woman or how close we may be as friends, she is not okay with me having a white wife. This is a barrier, a line in the sand that I can't cross."

Several white women were sympathetic to the dating plight of African American women, acknowledging that there are fewer black men than black women. One woman told me that her friend who was dating a black man did feel guilty that she was taking him away from a possible relationship with a black woman. Another woman said she had wondered what black women did to find husbands since so many black men are incarcerated. Finally, one woman asked me what I thought would happen to white women if more white men married outside their race. My answer to her was that if black women married white men in numbers equal to those of black men marrying white women, there wouldn't be as big a problem. It is the numerical imbalance that is at the crux of this issue.

Comments from white men who I shared my research with were also illuminating.

One man confessed that he had always found black women attractive, but didn't pursue any because of family and societal pressures. He had dated other darker skinned women, but felt because of historical circumstances, if he dated a black woman, he would be more self-conscious. Another man admitted that he had dated a black woman but always felt she really wanted a black husband. "I was okay until she could find her black Prince Charming." Two white men and one white woman told me that they had male family members married to black women and from what they could tell, these marriages were going as well as others in their families.

Finally, one white man told me that he was glad I was bringing this problem out in the open because maybe once people read about these interracial couples, it would reduce some prejudice.

CHAPTER 9

CONCLUDING THOUGHTS

Over the four years I spent interviewing participants for this study on black women who are dating, married to, or divorced from white men, I confirmed that romantic love and sexual attraction are not necessarily based on racial attributes. Indeed, the people I met were simply ordinary individuals who happened to meet and form relationships based on shared commonalities, allowing them to form bonds which were stronger than any external force to keep them apart. **In brief, these interracial relationships and marriages were essentially no different from same race ones.**

And that's the good news.

Crossing racial boundaries to form romantic relationships and marriages does require a certain consciousness that transcends historical narratives. Admittedly, this is not something everyone is able to do. However, for black women who would like to get married, interracial dating is an option which deserves serious consideration given the shortage of available and eligible black men. It is my hope that this book presents a realistic picture of what interracial dating and marriage looks like for anyone considering this alternative.

My research on dating, marriage and divorce allowed me to observe that there is no accounting for the vagaries in human attraction. While the black women and white men interviewed were easily identifiable as representative of their racial/ethnic group, there was no predicting who would be attractive to whom. The only commonality I found among most of the black women, as noted earlier, was a penchant for what can best be described as some Afro-centric marker, be it how they dressed, wore their hair, or random objects in their homes. Whether consciously or not, none of the women presented themselves as darker skinned versions of white women. What is meant by the latter statement is that none of the women wore fake straight hair, blue or green colored contact lenses, or were made up so as to appear lighter skinned than they were. Additionally, there was nothing 'hypersexual' about the women, meaning that none of them would have been described as overly curvaceous or resembling the Hottentot Venus due to having large hips or butts. Among the white men, there was a decided preference for curvy black women who were not thin, but also not overweight. Only three of the thirty black wives would be described as petite. A second observation was that among the younger couples, they were well aware of the historical demeaning relationships between black women and white men. However, this did not deter them from forming loving relationships in the present. As one black woman remarked, "How long do you hold on to past history? If you keep looking back, how can you go forward?" A white man asked me, "How much of the past do I have to be responsible for? It isn't my past...I have never disrespected any woman."

Among the black women who were dating white men, a common denominator was high self-esteem. The women were accomplished and had already achieved much in their lives. Undoubtedly this positive sense of self gave them the confidence to pursue romantic relationships outside their race. The white men who were interviewed were sensitive to racial nuances, at times expressing more concern for how their wives or girlfriends were feeling than the women felt was warranted. Most of the black women were accustomed to dealing with prejudice and racism, and thus inured to micro-aggressions that their boyfriends and husbands were experiencing due to their interracial relationship. As one black wife noted, "This [prejudice] is new for him, but it is something I have been dealing with for most of my life." However, one black wife was frustrated with her husband "because it didn't seem like he got it...or made light of it. David could always find a reason why something I thought was racist could be attributed to something else...but I stood my ground. No way was that not racist." What I found most impressive was that both partners were honestly communicating about their reactions and were willing to consider the other person's point of view, even if they didn't agree with it.

One of the many factors which contributes to a relationship surviving is how well the partners are empathetic and supportive of each other. One question a couple contemplating marriage should consider is "Does my intended make me a better person; do I make him/her a better person?" The response to this question will provide insight into the strength of the relationship and partner compatibility. For couples crossing the color line to marry, this question holds added weight because interracial marriages are not the social norm.

The black women who were divorced in this study experienced some remorse that their marriages ended, even if they had been the one to seek the separation. Most of the women did not attribute racial/ethnic differences as a major reason for their divorces. As noted earlier, of the two black-white marriage pairings, research suggests that black women married to white men divorce less frequently than black men married to white women.

I appreciated the candor of the white men interviewed for this book. Their stories were noteworthy for their sensitivity. I have not discovered any other research on the topic of interracial romantic relationships which address this issue exclusively from the perspective of white men. There are, however, numerous old studies which analyze why black men are attracted to white women. Early social psychological research on this topic primarily viewed the attraction as being pathological. Current research has largely debunked these theories. It is telling how little research has been done on why white men may be attracted to black women. Undoubtedly the American slave narrative and subsequent historical relationships between white men and black women have resulted in a topic that is too sensitive for many sociologists and psychologists to fully explore.

As I conclude this book, I would be remiss if I didn't note that in the public domain, including social media and television, there are more positive depictions of black women in loving romantic relationships with white men. Even as I write these words, one young biracial American woman, the product of an interracial marriage between a black woman and a white man, is soon to marry an English prince, a member of one of the most traditional and long-lasting monarchies in the world. When the epitome of white Anglo-Saxon culture and privilege approves of an interracial marriage, surely social attitudes regarding interracial relationships in America will continue to follow suit.

Finally, I want to thank all of the people who so graciously and honestly took the time to discuss their lives with me. Their willingness to share their most sensitive thoughts and intimate details with a relative stranger was heartwarming and appreciated. I trust I have done justice to them. Their stories demonstrate how far America has come and how much further it needs to progress before interracial dating, marriage and divorce are no longer viewed as the exception, but rather a norm in interpersonal relationships.

APPENDIX

Interracial Relationships Questionnaire

Questions for All Participants:

1. Male/Female

2. Racial/Ethnic Identification

3. Current Age

4. Education

5. Occupation

6. Income range

7. In what city/town did you grow up?

8. Religious affiliation growing up?

9. Religious affiliation now?

Additional Questions for Married Participants:

10. Age at current marriage

11. How many years have you been married?

12. Is this your: 1st, 2nd, or __marriage?

13. Where did you meet your spouse/?

14. How long did you date your spouse before marriage?

15. Was your spouse's race/ethnicity a concern for you?

16. Was your spouse's race/ethnicity a concern of other family members?

17. Did any family members object to your choice of spouse?

18. Did any close friends or associates object to your choice of spouse?

19. Do any of your family members object to your spouse due to his/her race ethnicity currently?

20. Do any of your close friends or associates object to your spouse due to his/her race or ethnicity currently?

21. Was this the first person of another racial/ethnic group that you dated?

22. How many other people of another racial/ethnic group did you date?

23. What attributes about your spouse initially attracted you to him/her?

24. How often do you visit your respective spouse's family?

25. What advice would you give to other couples contemplating an interracial marriage?

Additional Questions for Dating Participants:

1. How many people of another racial/ethnic group have you dated?

2. Do any of your family members or friends object to your dating outside of your race?

3. Where have you met your dating partners?

4. Did you make the first contact in interracial dating relationships?

5. What attributes initially attract you to someone?

6. Have you met your partner's family?

7. What advice would you give to other people contemplating dating interracially?

Additional Questions for Divorced Participants:

1. How many years were you married?

2. Where did you meet your former spouse?

3. How many years did you date your former spouse before marriage?

4. Did any close family members or friends of either of you object to your marriage?

5. Was your former spouse the first person of another race that you dated?

6. Briefly, describe the reason(s) for your divorce.

7. Did race or racial issues play a role in your divorce?

8. Do you have a relationship with your former spouse now?

9. Do you have a relationship with your former spouse's family now?

10. What advice would you give to other couples contemplating an interracial marriage?

FOOTNOTES

1. Lindsey, Linda L. 2010. Gender Roles: A Sociological Perspective, 5th ed. Glenview, Illinois: Pearson.

2. Pew Research Center Analysis of 2014-2015 American Community Survey: Intermarriage in The U.S. Fifty Years after Loving v Virginia.

3. 2010 Pew Research Center Report (U.S. Census Bureau's 2010 American Community Survey).

4. Goldman, N., C. Westhoff, and C. Hammerslough. 1984 Demography of the   Marriage Market in the United States. Population Index 50 (Spring): 5-25.

5. Alumna Advises Princeton Women to Find a Man on Campus. http://abcnews.go.com/GMA/video/ alumna-advices-princeton-women-find-man-campus-18848965

6. Ervin, K. (2017, September 11) Email interview.

7. Rush, A. (2018, March 2) Phone interview.

8. Judice, Y. (2018, February 25) Email interview.

9. Lowery, L. (2018, February 10) Personal interview.

10. Young, D. (2018, February 22) Phone interview.

11. Staples, Robert. 1981. The World of Black Singles: Changing Patterns of Male/Female Relations. Westport, CT: Greenwood Press

12. http://madamenoire.com/502861/online-dating-doesnt-work-for-black-women/10/

13. Pew Research Center Analysis of 2014-2015 American Community Survey: Intermarriage in the U.S. Fifty Years after Loving v Virginia

14. http://www.divorcesource.com/blog/interracial-marriage-and-divorce/

15. http://www.divorcesource.com/blog/interracial-marriage-and-divorce/

REFERENCES

Kotkin, Joel. 2010. The Next Hundred Million: America in 2050
New York, NY: The Penguin Group

Roberts, Robert E.T. 1994. Black-white Intermarriage in the United States. In *Inside the Mixed Marriage: Accounts Of Changing Attitudes, Patterns, and Perceptions of Cross-Cultural and Interracial Marriages*, ed. Walton R. Johnson and D. Michael Warren, Lanham, MD: University Press of America

Romano, Renee C. 2003. Race-Mixing: Black-White Marriage in Postwar America. Cambridge, MA: Harvard University Press.

Schwartz, Mary Ann, and BarBara M. Scott. 2000. Marriages and Families: Diversity And Change. 3rd ed. Upper Saddle, NJ: Prentice Hall.

ABOUT THE AUTHOR

Cheryl Y. Judice is the author of Interracial Marriages Between Black Women and White Men, (2008) the first academic text published on the experiences of black women in interracial marriages. She is a professor in the School of Education and Social Policy at Northwestern University. She holds a PhD and a MA in sociology from Northwestern University and a BA in psychology from Lake Forest College. She resides in Evanston with her husband, Hecky Powell, and two dogs. She has three adult children, two granddaughters, and writes a blog for Chicagonow.com titled, "Issues in Black and White."